Demography: A Very Short Introduction

VERY SHORT INTRODUCTIONS are for anyone wanting a stimulating and accessible way into a new subject. They are written by experts, and have been translated into more than 45 different languages.

The series began in 1995, and now covers a wide variety of topics in every discipline. The VSI library currently contains over 550 volumes—a Very Short Introduction to everything from Psychology and Philosophy of Science to American History and Relativity—and continues to grow in every subject area.

Very Short Introductions available now:

Available soon:

For more information visit our website

www.oup.com/vsi/

Sarah Harper

DEMOGRAPHY

A Very Short Introduction

OXFORD
UNIVERSITY PRESS

OXFORD
UNIVERSITY PRESS

Great Clarendon Street, Oxford, OX2 6DP,
United Kingdom

Oxford University Press is a department of the University of Oxford.
It furthers the University's objective of excellence in research, scholarship,
and education by publishing worldwide. Oxford is a registered trade mark of
Oxford University Press in the UK and in certain other countries

Published in the United States of America by Oxford University Press
198 Madison Avenue, New York, NY 10016, United States of America

British Library Cataloguing in Publication Data
Data available

Library of Congress Control Number: 2018931300

ISBN 978-0-19-872573-2

Printed in Great Britain by
Ashford Colour Press Ltd, Gosport, Hampshire

For Caroline

Contents

Demography

List of illustrations

List of tables

Chapter 1
Demography is destiny ... or not

In the background to the emergence of the First World War, the alliance between France and Russia played a crucial role. While political allegiances had led to this, it is also recognized that it was France losing the demographic race with Germany which also promoted the alliance. France received a huge reserve of Russian manpower in return for sending its capital and technology. Twenty-first-century Britain's multicultural society emerged from its declining ability to replace its population by births alone during the second half of the 20th century. This encouraged an exchange of migrant labour from its former colonies in return for capital transfers. Japan's early economic success has been partially explained by its high-density population which enabled technology transfer to rapidly occur. Political alliances, cultural change, and economic growth can be all attributed in part to the demographic structure of the nations involved.

The origin of the concept that 'demography is destiny' is contested. While few would maintain quite such a deterministic stance, it is increasingly recognized that population change plays a key role in our political systems, economies, and societies at the local, national, regional, and global level.

While there are many subjects which are interested in people, such as anthropology, sociology, and psychology, demography has at its core the notion of drivers of population change, namely mortality, fertility, and migration, and how these then interact to change populations. The interaction of these demographic drivers has led to various outcomes in terms of population size, composition, density, and distribution, which vary within and between countries and regions. These then have a significant impact on the societies and communities which they form, and also on the individuals who make up those societies and communities. For example, the birth cohort or generation into which each person is born, the demographic composition of that cohort, and its relation to those born at the same time in other places, and before and after, strongly influence individual life chances. Additionally there are impacts upon the economic and political structures within which that life is lived, structuring access to social and natural resources such as food, water, education, jobs, sexual partners, and even the length of an individual's life.

England, the mid-17th century: a time of renewal and discovery, a time of plague and death. The coincidence of these two conditions led to the founding of demography. The Royal Society was established in 1660 dedicated to 'empirical observation and experiment'; Newton and colleagues at Cambridge were developing calculus, the science of mechanics, and the theory of gravity. The identification of mathematical formulae which explained God's work in physics and the physical world was a natural path to discovering further formulae which would explain his plan for the human body. All around was death, emanating from the relentless spread of the Plague. The *Bills of Mortality* which published weekly numbers of London burials provided the perfect source from which to explore the laws of life and death programmed into the world at God's creation. The use of this data by the merchant John Graunt to create the first primitive life table in 1662 was the original piece of research in demography. The laws of earth, the sea, and the sky had been joined by a mathematical law of life and death. While demography has expanded over the centuries to encompass wide-ranging theories and methodologies which explore the basic tenets of how populations grow, reproduce, and change, still within its heart remains the search for mathematical laws which may explain the length of human lives; a search which it now shares with fellow scientists in mathematics, evolutionary biology, and genetics.

Contemporary demography may be divided into three separate areas of study. First is the study of the characteristics of past or current populations, with regard to their size and make-up. Particular interest is shown in the criteria of age, sex, marital status, education, spatial distribution, ethnicity, and socio-economic group. Second is an interest in the different processes which directly influence this composition, primarily fertility, mortality, and migration, sometimes known as the demographic drivers. The third area concerns the relationship between these static characteristics and dynamic processes and the social, economic, and cultural environments within which they interact.

Current authors argue that modern demography holds a special place within the social sciences. Unlike many other social disciplines, such as sociology or psychology, the units of analysis are clear—people. Furthermore, the laws governing the human action of the main demographic processes, reproduction and death—fertility and mortality—are more regular than many other behavioural processes. Third, contemporary demography is a true interdisciplinary discipline, as it relies heavily on other social sciences to interpret demographic outcomes.

In this Very Short Introduction I shall start by exploring the way in which the global population evolved over time and space, experiencing a steady though small increase for thousands of years, until it transitioned around 200 years ago and global population grew dramatically. At the end of the last ice age 20,000 years ago there are estimated to have been around 1 million *Homo sapiens* scattered across Europe, Africa, and Asia.

The next 15,000 years saw a dramatic evolution in human economy and society with the emergence of agriculture, settled dwelling, and civilizations. By 5000 BC the world population had reached an estimated 5 million and each continent was now settled. It took a further 7,000 years for the human population to reach 1 billion by around AD 1800.

The advent of urbanization and industrialization led to a steady increase in population numbers. From 1700, the death rate began a long gradual decline: trade, agricultural, and industrial revolutions increased standards of living, and public health initiatives significantly reduced infant and child mortality. The population doubled to 2 billion by the early 1900s (around 1930) and within fifty years had doubled again to 4 billion (1975), and had reached 6 billion by the millennium. It now stands at some 7 billion and is projected to reach around 10 billion during this century.

I shall then look at the development of the discipline of demography, considering who the main theorists were, why they became interested in demography, and how they shaped the discipline across the centuries. As I have described, formal study of demography may be traced back to Graunt in the mid-17th century with his primitive life tables. Others took up the task and by the 19th century mathematical estimations were sophisticated and well recognized. Theoretically, it was Malthus who hypothesized the implications of unchecked population growth and is thus seen by many as the true founder of demographic studies.

One of the major debates has been around the demographic transition—or transitions. This is the series of changes that occur as countries evolve from a stable state of high mortality balanced by high fertility to one of low mortality and low fertility. The timing and drivers of this transition are heatedly contested by the theorists. We shall explore the tools and materials used by demographers to understand these processes.

By the early 20th century, demography was recognized as a separate field of study, with the first university courses being taught, key theorists recognized, and a clear set of methods and techniques developed. Alongside this we shall consider the emergence of new demographic sub-disciplines. Recent decades have seen both the inclusion of demography within other disciplines (e.g. sociology, history, economics) as an area of study, and the development of sub-disciplines. Bio-demography, population economics, population geography, social demography, and anthropological demography, all now form part of a broad field of population studies which analyse the relationships between economic, social, cultural, and biological processes influencing a population. This has enabled a multi-disciplinary approach to be taken which can address a variety of contemporary issues and make use of the predictive power of demography to look into the future.

Do all countries have population policies? We shall consider some of these, before addressing some key population challenges of the 21st century. Will fertility rates fall to replacement in sub-Saharan Africa? And what will be the consequences if they do not? What is the relationship between environment, population, and consumption in different parts of the world? How will we feed and provide water for the projected 9 or 10 billion of us by 2050? What will be the impact of the upcoming ageing of the world's population?

Demography, at its core a mathematical science, is addressing some of these grand challenges. Demography may not be destiny, but it can provide the scientific evidence needed to guide governments and policy makers across the 21st century.

Chapter 2
From 55,000 to 7 billion

The human population as we understand it today commenced around a million years ago; 1.2 million years ago there were some 55,000 humans from which all today's human population descended. This included several species such as *Homo ergaster* in Africa and *Homo erectus* in East Asia. New genetic evidence is transforming our understanding of human evolution. This data suggests that all modern humans, African and non-African alike, descend from one homogeneous ancestral population in the last 100,000 years. This goes against earlier theories that African separated from non-African populations much earlier.

In addition, this data also suggests that after *Homo sapiens* left Africa some 60,000 years ago the sharing of genetic material through interbreeding between African and non-African populations continued until 20,000–40,000 years ago.

In addition, comprehensive dating of bones and tools suggests that modern humans arrived in Europe as early as 45,000 years ago and lived alongside Neanderthals for up to 5,000 years and may even have exchanged ideas and culture. There is also genetic evidence that these human populations subsequently interbred with Neanderthals and that modern European people in particular contain up to 5 per cent Neanderthal DNA. Researchers suggest that Neanderthals declined in numbers over thousands of years

Box 1 Did modern humans slaughter Neanderthal man to become the dominant species?

There has long been speculation that modern humans arriving in Europe from Africa introduced fatal African diseases and hunted down and slaughtered the resident Neanderthals, causing their extinction within 500 years. Researchers now believe that the two species lived together for as long as 5,000 years, hunting the same animals, collecting the same plants, and exchanging ideas, technology, and culture. They even interbred, leading to Neanderthal DNA in modern European populations. Both archaeological and genetic evidence shows that when modern humans arrived in Europe from Africa, the Neanderthals were already in decline, and were probably unable to survive the harsh climatic change that occurred throughout Europe some 40,000 years ago.

while at the same time modern humans increased in number. A period of extremely cold weather around 40,000 years ago might have proved too much for the dwindling population numbers, and led to their final extinction (Box 1).

By 30000 BC *Homo sapiens* are recognized to be the only type of human left on the planet. At the end of the last ice age (last glacial maximum) some 20,000 years ago, the time of the Palaeolithic Age, there were estimated to be around 1 million people, scattered across Europe, Africa, and Asia. Genetic evidence suggests that the European population may have shrunk considerably on first leaving Africa. Humans had reached Australia, but probably not the Americas.

Rapid economic and social evolution

The next 15,000 years saw a dramatic evolution in human economy and society with the emergence of agriculture, settled dwelling, and civilizations. Around 10,000 years ago there was a period of global warming, the ice sheets melted and retreated, and we entered the Holocene period, in which we still live today. Initially this led to the cultural periods of Mesolithic hunter-gatherers and Neolithic agriculturalists, and it is argued that this agricultural development supported sustained population growth at this time. The dramatic transformation of the Neolithic Revolution around 10000 BC, sometimes termed the Neolithic Demographic Transition, occurred whereby populations moved from a nomadic hunter-gathering to sedentary agriculture. This transition appears to have occurred independently across continents and time—from Europe and the Middle East, to the Near East, China, and Mesoamerica. The former Palaeolithic hunter-gatherers mostly existed in small independent groups vulnerable to local variations in food supply. Neolithic agriculturalists formed larger, denser concentrations of population who could withstand seasonal times of famine through the building up of surpluses.

The classic theory explaining the sudden expansion in population during this production transition assumes that the innovation and diffusion of new techniques of production, the cultivation of easily stored nutritional grains, and the domestication of animals expanded the availability of food and protected populations from nutritional stress. As a result health improved, mortality declined, and the population grew.

This theory has been questioned, however, by others who suggest that in fact mortality increased, rather than declined, and it was only the increase in fertility levels which led to population growth. Here it is argued that as people turned from a mixed diet of fruits and vegetables and meat to a high reliance on grains, the nutritional value of their diet decreased. In addition it is proposed that the higher-density living of settled agriculture populations allowed the spread of parasites and infectious diseases. Thus the nutritionally weaker agriculturalists had high rates of morbidity and lower life expectancies than the hunter-gatherers who preceded them.

However, the transition from nomadic to settled ways of living increased fertility. Modern anthropological studies in Africa, for example, have indicated that women who have taken up settled agriculture have shorter spacing between childbirths than their contemporaries who still remain hunter-gatherers. For nomadic peoples it is burdensome to continually move around with babies and infants, while child labour is a valuable asset to farming. Regardless of the theory, the population increased considerably and by 5000 BC the world population had reached an estimated 5 million and each continent was now settled (Box 2).

These two theories both explore the influence of economic and social ways of life on the behaviour of the populations involved. It is also possible that the demography itself influenced people's behaviour. For example, it may be argued that around 10,000 years ago population pressure on the land available for hunting and gathering forced populations to cultivate food as well as gather it, in order to make the available land more productive. It is suggested that hunter-gatherers knew how to grow crops as well as to gather, but it was not until they needed to switch to cultivation due to population pressure that this transition occurred. Such arguments are supported by evidence that

Box 2 Are there more humans alive today than have ever lived?

Although it is difficult to estimate historical population figures the Population Reference Bureau estimates that about 107 billion people have ever lived. There are currently 7 billion people alive today, which means that for every living person fifteen have lived before and died. Demographers believe that by the time of Christ the planet had already been home to over 7 billion people.

the move to agriculture required a greater workload than hunting and gathering and thus would only have been adopted under necessity.

Over the subsequent 5,000 years the Neolithic transition allowed the doubling of the population each two millennia, arriving at a quarter of a billion by the time of Christ. This was a considerable increase in growth from the previous 25,000 years of humankind, in which the population had needed nearly 10,000 years to double each time. Many scholars link this growth with the emergence of new technologies, allowing the diffusion of crops, animals, and inventions, and also people, along a fertile geographical axis spreading across Eurasia. The invention of the wheel, for example, in South-East Asia in around 3000 BC transformed transportation, allowing the rapid movement of people and goods along newly created roads. Writing emerged in both Mesopotamia and China at around the same time, leading to the spread of ideas and innovations. Both of these led to the creation of new civilizations and large territorial empires—the Ottoman Empire, Egyptian Kingdoms, Roman Empire, and Chinese Dynasty, for example. At its height the Roman Empire probably comprised some 50 million people, with some suggesting that Rome itself held over 1 million people. There was probably an equivalent population in India and China. Large cities emerged developing systems of governance and control over growing populations. These supported wide-scale technological innovations such as irrigation systems leading to vastly improved food supplies, regulation of water supplies, drainage and sanitation systems, and mathematical and accounting mechanisms which regulated trade. Though population growth was supported by these new innovations, it was also still vulnerable to disease, famine, and changes in the climate, which kept rapid population growth in check.

The next one and a half thousand years saw huge fluctuations in population growth. It appears that there was little increase in

10

world population size between AD 500 and 900, followed by growth over the next 400 years in many parts of the world. Roman Britain stood at around 1 million at the dawn of the millennium but was of the same population a thousand years later when the Doomsday Book was written. The first three centuries of the second millennium heralded a period of steady growth and population expansion in many parts. The European and African populations doubled, and those in Asia and the Americas by 1.5. Britain's population, for example, grew rapidly under the Normans, increasing some fourfold to 4 million. Evidence from Ceylon suggests rapid growth supported by sophisticated agricultural systems, reaching a high in the 12th century. China probably grew from 70 million at the beginning of the millennium, to 120 million by the 12th century.

During the 1300s, however, with the exception of the Americas, these populations then shrank back. It may have been a change in global climate—the European climate was particularly unfavourable during this time, for example—or a natural brake on population growth due to population pressure, or simply a coincidence. The Black Death of the 14th century, a pandemic plague which spread from the Gobi desert to China, India, the Middle East, and Europe, cut back the European population by one-third. This was followed by a period of restrained growth for 300 years.

In the 1500s the European discovery of the Americas had a catastrophic effect on the indigenous populations. The Native Americans and the civilizations of the Aztecs in the North and the Incas in the South were decimated by disease, famine, and war. From 1600 Asia experienced periods of growth and then stagnation. Japan, which tripled its population between 1600 and 1700, then rapidly declined. Likewise China doubled its population between 1700 and 1800 and then slowed again. A great trading empire, China turned inwards, failing to industrialize like its European neighbours, and losing out on the subsequent European demographic boom of the 19th century.

Steady expansion

Then at the end of the 18th century, a change occurred in Europe. The boom and bust of population growth steadied. The high mortality and high fertility rates started to fall. Women who had lost up to half their babies and children before they reached reproductive age no longer had to bear five or six children just to replace the parents. Deaths across the life course were reduced. Europe had entered the demographic transition.

By the end of the 18th century, after 30,000 years of human habitation, world population had reached 1 billion, scattered across all regions. Within 100 years over half the babies born would make it to reproductive age, and with continuous increase in life expectancy, the world population would commence its steady, continuous growth. By 1930 world population had doubled to reach 2 billion people, doubled again to 4 billion by 1975, and is predicted to double again by around 2030. Distribution of this population has also changed. Asia consistently held two-thirds of the world population until 1900, when its share of the world population declined to 57 per cent. Europe increased to reach 25 per cent by 1900 before slipping back considerably to under 10 per cent by the end of the century. Africa has remained at around 15 per cent and the Americas at around 10 per cent.

Looking forward it is predicted that there will be an overall increase in those living in Asia and Africa and a continued fall in European and North American populations; 97 per cent of all population growth to 2050 is predicted to occur in the emerging economies, predominantly in Asia and Latin America, and the least developed countries, mainly in sub-Saharan Africa. Asia will comprise 55 per cent of the world population by 2050 at 5 billion, while Europe will decline from 740 to 709 million, only around 7 per cent of the global population.

In addition, rural-to-urban migration, combined with natural increase, is leading to a disproportionate increase in urban population, especially in less developed countries. At the end of the 19th century only 10 per cent of the world's population lived in urban areas. By 1950, the urban population stood at 29 per cent, reaching over 50 per cent by the millennium and predicted to reach 75 per cent by 2025. Urban areas are also increasing in size. In 1950, only two cities, Tokyo and New York, were over 10 million people. There are currently twenty-eight mega-cities with over 10 million. It is predicted that by 2030, there could be forty-one urban areas with over 10 million people. Eight of these urban areas would hold over 20 million people each, with all but two in developed regions.

The age composition of the world is also changing. By the measure of more people over 60 than under 15, Europe reached maturity at the turn of the millennium. By 2050 the proportion of young people in Asia will have fallen and there will be more than 1 billion people over 60, 20 per cent of the population, compared to less than 1 billion under 15, 19 per cent of the population. Similarly, Latin America and the Caribbean will reach 20 per cent age 60 and over by 2040, while those under 15 will fall to 19 per cent. Indeed by 2050 there will for the first time be the same number of old as young in the world—with 2 billion of each—each accounting for 21 per cent of the world's population. Africa, however, will continue to grow and remain young. It is projected to double in size by 2050 from 1 to 2.3 billion, with one-third of its population remaining under 15.

As the French demographer Livi Bacci has stated, 'The million inhabitants of the Palaeolithic Age, the 10 million of the Neolithic Age, the 100 million of the Bronze Age, the billion of the Industrial Revolution, or the 10 billion we may attain at the end of the twenty-first century certainly represent more than simple demographic growth.'

Chapter 3
The fathers of demographic thought

Demographic ideas can be traced back to antiquity. The term 'demography' comes from the Greek 'demos' meaning the common people of an ancient Greek state and all ancient civilizations developed a means of describing the people and composition of their societies. It is, however, generally accepted that demography originated in the middle of the 17th century with the English statistician, John Graunt, as its founder. It may even be argued that demography has an exact date of birth, 27 February 1662, when Graunt's *Observations* were first published. For while there were population censuses well before this date, including information about numbers of deaths and births, this was the first attempt to examine statistical regularities inherent within these numbers.

Yet what is striking, when considering the theorists who founded and developed the study of 'demography', is the diversity of their social and academic backgrounds. Beginning in the 17th century with an inquisitive and pragmatic merchant and followed by astrologers, philosophers, statisticians, engineers, and economists, the theorists discussed in this chapter are brought together by their shared interest in the study of people. As diverse as their backgrounds are the motivations that drove their research. What is viewed today as an academic field was stimulated by market research, personal economic gain, and in many cases simply occurred as a result of chance events and circumstances.

England's Royal Society played an important role in demography's early development. The Royal Society for the Improvement of Natural Knowledge was established in 1660, dedicated to 'empirical observation and experiment, first to the study of the natural world and technology, and then to the study of society'. An important shift occurred in the 20th century when demography became an academic subject, first as part of mathematics and statistics, and university courses commenced, demographers were trained, and demography became recognized as a separate field of study; in 1928 the International Union for the Scientific Investigation of Population Problems was established.

John Graunt (1620–1674)

The formal study of demography can be traced to the English 'statistician' John Graunt, born in London on 24 April 1620. Little is known about his education, although it is assumed that he did not attend university. Despite the lack of a formal education, Graunt's biographer John Aubrey describes him as an ingenious and studious person, and it is known that Graunt taught himself French and Latin. John Graunt followed his father, Henry Graunt, into haberdashery and by 1666 he was an opulent London haberdashery merchant. It was Graunt's interest in the composition of his potential customer base which led him to explore the characteristics of the population of London. Graunt studied the London parish records and in 1662 published his *Natural and Political Observations Made Upon the Bills of Mortality* containing the first, primitive life table (see Table 1) which clearly and concisely presented data from the different parish churches of London, which collected and recorded the information about their congregations. Whilst Graunt's method might be seen today as simplistic it enabled him to extract some interesting population trends. For example, his analysis revealed that both birth rates and mortality rates were higher in males than in females. So, although more men were being born, fewer were reaching 'old age'. Graunt was thus able to show that on

Table 1 Graunt's life table

Age interval	Prop. deaths in interval	Prop. surviving till start of interval
0–6	0.36	1.00
7–16	0.24	0.64
17–26	0.15	0.40
27–36	0.09	0.25
37–46	0.06	0.16
47–56	0.04	0.10
57–66	0.03	0.06
67–76	0.02	0.03

balance there were a fairly even number of adult males and females in the population.

Graunt's analysis also enabled him to 'estimate roughly the number of men currently of military age, the number of women of childbearing age, the total number of families, and even the population of London'. He could also estimate the probability of survival to each age with his data revealing that the chance of death at 50 was the same as the chance of death at 20. From this Graunt deduced that these deaths could not be solely age related and suggested that the 'plague' must be the overriding factor. The 'plague', or more likely a variety of different 'plagues', had been endemic in London for many years and was an important concern for King Charles II, who was working on a system to prevent the spread of plague in London. On 27 February 1662, 'the birthday of demography', Graunt presented his life table to the Royal Society. Two months later, on 26 April, Graunt became a member of the Royal Society on the personal recommendation of the king.

Although Graunt is widely considered today to be the founder of demography, he died in 1674 bankrupt and disgraced. His conversion, late in life, from Calvinism to Catholicism, loss of his business in the 1666 Great Fire of London, and slanderous gossip concerning his (unlikely) involvement in the promotion of the fire, led to his fall from favour. Following his death attempt was made to reattribute his 'Bills of Mortality' to Graunt's social acquaintance, Sir William Petty. Whilst Petty certainly did not write Graunt's 'Bills of Mortality' he built upon Graunt's founding achievements. Whilst recognition and praise may have waned during Graunt's lifetime, his way of thinking and interest in the population paved the way for demographers today. Graunt's tables led to the universal registrations of births, marriages, and causes of death, and he can rightly be named the Founder of Demography.

Sir William Petty (1623–1687)

Sir William Petty shared with Graunt an inquisitive spirit. Their appetite for knowledge and scientific enquiry is characteristic of the 17th century as epitomized in the establishment of the Royal Society, of which Petty was a founding member. Petty started life even more disadvantaged than Graunt, born the son of a poor Hampshire cloth-worker. However, wealth and power followed—he was educated at the universities of Leiden, Paris, and Oxford, held professorships in anatomy at Oxford and music in London, became a Member of Parliament, and was knighted in 1661 by King Charles II.

At the age of 13 years, Petty voyaged to sea as a cabin boy. But following an accident in which he broke his leg, he was put ashore in France. Taking the opportunity, Petty applied to a Jesuit University to read Latin, and received an excellent education in both languages and mathematics. Leaving France, Petty studied medicine in Holland, and anatomy in Paris. Here Petty became part of a circle of scientists and philosopher-mathematicians which included both Pascal and Descartes. The following year, 1646, he returned to England to study medicine at Oxford University. Within five years another opportunity had presented itself, and he became the 'physician-in-chief of Cromwell's army in Ireland'. Upon arriving in Ireland Petty made another move, usurping his friend Dr Benjamin Worsley, to become the surveyor-general of Cromwell's Irish lands. Within twenty years, Petty had risen from a poor cabin boy to a powerful owner of around 100,000 acres of confiscated Irish land.

Petty's important contribution to demography also occurred in 1662, when he published his 'Treatise of Taxes and Contributions' in the same year as Graunt published his life tables. Petty's work had a strong economic focus, examining the role of the state in the economy, touching on the labour theory of value, and extrapolating an estimate of community economic loss caused by deaths from mortality rates. Petty is thus viewed as one of the originators of political arithmetic, which he defined as 'the art of reasoning by figures upon things relating to government', and originated many of the concepts that are still used in economics today, coining the term 'full employment', for example.

Edmond Halley (1656–1742)

Edmond Halley is probably better known for his work in astronomy than for his contribution to demography. He is particularly known for calculating the orbit of the comet later named 'Halley's Comet'. As with Sir William Petty, Halley's expertise was multi-disciplinary. In addition to studying astronomy, Halley pursued cartography, publishing the first ever meteorological chart, and was involved in the publishing of Isaac Newton's *Mathematical Principles of Natural Philosophy*, 1687. Importantly for demography, Halley became interested in mortality tables, which laid the foundation for the future production of actuarial tables in life insurance.

Edmond Halley was born on 8 November 1656 in Shoreditch, near London. Halley's father was a successful soap-maker who, like John Graunt, lost much of his business in the 1666 Fire of London. Fortunately, Halley's father could still afford for Edmond to be privately tutored at home and then to attend St Paul's school in London. He also promoted and funded Edmond's pursuit of astronomy as a hobby, buying him the necessary astrological instruments. When Halley was admitted to Queen's College, Oxford in 1673, at the age of 17, he was already an 'expert astronomer'. He was elected to the Royal Society in November 1678, at the age of only 22, one of its youngest fellows. Halley became the Editor of the Royal Society's *Philosophical Transactions* in 1685, where he made his main contribution to demography through his interest in mortality tables, publishing the mortality tables for the city of Breslau, now Wrocław, Poland, in 1693, one of the earliest works to relate mortality and age in a population. However, astronomy remained Halley's foremost interest and in 1697 he left England to sail to Britain's southernmost territory, St Helena, to map the stars of the southern hemisphere, funded by his great supporter—Charles II.

Richard Price (1723–1791)

Richard Price was born in 1723, the first of our theorists not to be under the patronage of King Charles II. During Price's lifetime the *Encyclopaedia Britannica* was first published, in 1771, evidence of a continued commitment to discovery. Price's circle of friends further reflect the dynamism of the time and include the British Prime Minister William Pitt, Benjamin Franklin, and the philosopher of the enlightenment, David Hume. Price's major contribution to demography was his founding of a scientific system for life insurance and old-age pensions.

Price worked as a Congregational minister, following in the footsteps of his father, the Reverend Rice Price. Richard Price was a 'Dissenter' who did not follow the established, national church, choosing instead to minister to Presbyterians. He was an ardent supporter of the French and American Revolutions and was well known in his day for his controversial views, often attracting large crowds when he preached. Price eulogized the French Revolution in a celebrated sermon, 'A Discourse on the Love of Our Country' (1789), to which Edmund Burke's *Reflections on the Revolution in France* was a reply. Like both Petty and Halley, Price's scientific interests were diverse. He was interested in electricity and followed the work of his friend Joseph Priestley, the discoverer of oxygen.

Price's major contribution to demography occurred as a consequence of the death of an acquaintance, Mr Bayes. His grieving family asked if Price could examine the recently deceased's papers, written on a variety of subjects. Price had been elected to the Royal Society in 1765 for his work on probability and realized the importance of Bayes's 'Essay toward Solving a Problem in the Doctrine of Chances', sharing it with the Royal Society. Bayes's papers seem to have been the catalyst to Price's engagement in insurance, demography, and financial and political reform. In 1769 Price wrote a letter to Benjamin Franklin commenting on 'the expectation of lives, the increase of mankind, and the population of London'. His observations were published in the *Philosophical Transactions of the Royal Society* later the same year.

Price's scientific system for life insurance and old-age pensions was published in *Observations on Reversionary Payments* in 1771. This book, along with *An Appeal to the Public on the Subject of the National Debt*, published the following year, led William Pitt to re-establish the sinking fund to extinguish England's national debt. Price was awarded the freedom of the City of London in 1776 and was invited by the US Congress to advise them on finances two years later. Together with George Washington he was made LL.D. by Yale College in 1781.

Thomas Malthus (1766–1834)

It is 1798, the world population has more or less reached 1 billion, but no one knows that yet. And the founder of modern demographic studies, Thomas Malthus speaks:

> The constant effort towards population…increases the number of people before the means of subsistence are increased. The food therefore which before supported seven millions must now be divided among seven millions and a half or eight millions. The poor consequently must live much worse, and many of them be reduced to severe distress.

This was the time of the Irish Rebellion, the aftermath of the French Revolution, Napoleon's fleet was at sea, his destination unknown, unrest and famine on land. The summer of 1798 followed a decade of political tumult. Food riots had crippled England between 1794 and 1796 as poor harvests and high food prices threatened the rural poor. Labour riots erupted with the widespread breaking of the new machinery that threatened the livelihoods of rural craftsmen. The conditions of the poor, the unrest of the working man, the spread of radicalism all combined to spur Malthus on to write his thesis. Malthus was a scientist, nature was composed of laws, and the scientist's role was to discover and elucidate them for the good of mankind.

Malthus was born on 13 February 1766 into a prosperous family. Like Richard Price, Malthus's father was an acquaintance of David Hume and a follower of the philosophies of enlightenment. Malthus, described as an 'economic pessimist', was ideologically divergent to both his father and to Price. Whilst Price supported the French Revolution, Malthus's beliefs can be seen as a reaction against it.

Malthus was educated at home before being admitted to Jesus College, Cambridge in 1784, where he excelled academically.

He earned his Master of Arts degree in 1791, was elected a fellow of Jesus College in 1793, and took holy orders in 1797. In 1805 Malthus became a professor of history and political economy at the East India Company's college at Haileybury, Hertfordshire. It was the first time in Great Britain that the world's political economy had been used to designate an academic office. In 1819 Malthus was elected a fellow of the Royal Society.

In 1798 Malthus published anonymously the first edition of *An Essay on the Principle of Population as It Affects the Future Improvement of Society, with Remarks on the Speculations of Mr. Godwin, M. Condorcet, and Other Writers*. Malthus argued that infinite human hopes for social happiness must be vain, for population will always tend to outrun the growth of production.

Malthus's premises were based on a series of postulates. Food is necessary to the existence of man; the passion between the sexes is necessary and will remain in its present state; the population will increase geometrically, food will increase at the smaller arithmetic ratio. Currently population growth was restrained by 'positive checks'—war, famine, pestilence. It was important that man moved to a series of 'preventative checks'—restraint, reason, and foresight—to limit population, alleviate suffering, and improve the well-being of mankind.

His position on the human condition was heavily influenced by the doctrines of the French Revolution, and by the prevailing thought—held by such as Mr Godwin—that rational people would eventually live prosperously and harmoniously without laws and institutions. In contrast, Malthus was essentially an empiricist and took as his starting point the harsh realities of the time. His reaction developed in the tradition of British economics, which would today be considered sociological. The Malthusian theory of population was, nevertheless, incorporated into theoretical systems of economics. It acted as a brake on economic optimism, helped to justify a theory of wages based on the wage earners' minimum cost of subsistence, and discouraged traditional forms of charity. The Malthusian theory of population made a strong and immediate impact on British social policy. There was a prevailing belief that high birth rates added to national wealth. Malthus, however, believed that to maximize wealth, a nation had to balance 'the power to produce and the will to consume'.

Malthus was of course unaware that he inhabited a world which was on a tipping point. Europe was about to experience new availability of land both within the continent and in new lands overseas which would alleviate rural population pressure through migration, and new sources of food, aided by improved transportation. Emanating from France, birth control was slowly to spread forth across the region; thus while the passion between the sexes might not be controlled, the outcome—births—could be. New technologies were about to transform agricultural production, thus significantly increasing food production, and to provide new sources of labour for the working man. The European demographic transition was about to commence. While Malthus is criticized for his failure to anticipate that the agricultural revolution, emigration, and birth control would avert his predictions of disastrous overpopulation, he understood the dynamics of the population drivers of fertility and mortality and laid the basis for modern population studies.

From John Graunt to Thomas Malthus these early pioneering individuals helped to shape our understanding of the study of populations. They drew attention to the fact that studying people from a demographic perspective was as important as understanding them from a medical perspective (Richard Price) or exploring the planet that they live on (Edmond Halley). These foundations were central to developing the relationship between analytical reasoning, numerical problems, and arithmetical records. Their work, while inseparable from the commercial, legal, and religious idioms of risk and its evaluation, may be argued as forming the foundations of modern probability.

Chapter 4
The entrance of statistics and mathematical models

By the 19th century the study of 'demography' had developed from John Graunt's primitive life table to the complex statistical laws and theories of Gompertz and Makeham. The Royal Society was still to play a part in demography's evolution, though this was to wane and almost disappear as the focus of methodological development moved away from Britain to Europe, the USA, and Australia, and with the formation of the International Union for the Scientific Investigation of Population Problems in 1927 a professional body was established to mould future developments.

While Malthus's theory of the Principle of Population now holds little relevance, the Gompertz–Makeham law of mortality, the first parametric model of human mortality, is still valid today. This states that the death rate is the sum of an age-independent component (the Makeham term) and an age-dependent component (Gompertz function) which increases exponentially with age. The men responsible for this law are Benjamin Gompertz and William Makeham.

Benjamin Gompertz (1779–1865)

Gompertz was born on 5 March 1779 into a family of Jewish merchants who had settled in England from Holland. As a Jew he was unable to attend university and, as a consequence, he was self-educated. Gompertz developed a passion for mathematics, which he learnt 'by reading Newton and Maclaurin'. Gompertz's mathematical education greatly benefited from his joining the Spitalfields Mathematical Society (which later became the London Mathematical Society) at the age of 18. The anecdote surrounding Gompertz joining the London Mathematical Society is that he passed by a poor bookkeeper's shop. The owner, John Griffiths, was a gifted mathematician whom Gompertz was pleased to meet. The two talked and Gompertz asked for lessons from Griffiths. Griffiths replied that Gompertz was probably more adept to give the lessons and suggested that he join the Society. Gompertz applied and was elected—the youngest member ever. Thirteen years later, in 1810, Gompertz joined the stock exchange, becoming a Fellow of the Royal Society in 1819.

Gompertz's greatest contribution to demography came in the form of 'Gompertz's Law of Mortality', 1825. While he was not the first to attempt a mathematical formulation of the laws of mortality, Gompertz argued that 'It is possible that death may be the consequence of two generally co-existing causes; the one, chance, without previous disposition to death or deterioration; the other, a deterioration, or an increased inability to withstand destruction,' and that mankind was 'continually gaining seeds of indisposition, or in other words, an increasing liability to death'. Gompertz deduced that a form of the following equation could be used to capture the force of mortality:

$$q_x = B \cdot C^x$$

where q is the probability of dying at exact age x, and B and C are constants.

Gompertz's law showed that the mortality rate increases in a geometric progression. Hence, when death rates are plotted on a logarithmic scale, a straight line known as the Gompertz function is obtained. In 1834 Gompertz became a founding member of the Royal Statistical Society.

William Makeham (1826–1891)

Makeham's greatest contribution to demography was his modification to Gompertz's 'Law of Mortality' (1825). Over forty years after Gompertz had presented his findings to the Royal Society Makeham suggested the following alteration:

$$q_x = A + B \cdot C^x$$

'…in which the third constant, A, is used to represent the influence of causes of death not dependant on age'. Thus while Gompertz argued that mortality rates grow exponentially with age, Makeham's contribution consists in the addition of an age-independent constant that, on the one hand, accounts for mortality that is not related to ageing and, on the other hand, introduces an additional third parameter that improves the model. Makeham's Law is thus 'an actuarial rule: the mortality risk of a person at any age over 20 is equal to a constant plus a simple exponential function of the age'.

The period 1860–1910 is viewed as a time of transition wherein demography emerged from statistics. An international group of demographers—Lambert Adolphe Jacques Quételet, William Farr, Louis-Adolphe and Jacques Bertillon, Joseph Körösi, Anders Nicolai Kiaer, Richard Böckh, Wilhelm Lexis, and Luigi Bodio—all contributed significantly to the development of demography and demographic methods and analysis.

William Farr (1807–1883)

William Farr was a British epidemiologist, regarded as one of the founders of medical statistics. Born in Shropshire to poor parents, his patronage by a local landowner enabled him to gain an education and he studied medicine at University College

London. When the General Register Office was established in England and Wales in 1838 William Farr was appointed compiler of statistical abstracts and later Superintendent of the Statistical Department. A Fellow of the Royal Society, he was also involved in the Social Science Association from its foundation in 1857. Farr was appointed Assistant Commissioner of the censuses of 1851, 1861, and 1871 and wrote the Census Reports of these years including the construction of the first English life table. This allowed him full access to the main sources of epidemiological and demographic data for England and Wales.

Farr's role in the studies of cholera in the three epidemics between 1848 and 1867 made a significant contribution to the method of surveillance in controlling the disease. During the pandemic of 1848–9 Farr organized an intensive study of the cholera returns throughout England and Wales. He published data showing mortality by areas of London according to their water supplies which revealed that areas most contaminated with sewage from the River Thames experienced the highest mortality. He then publicly called on the water companies to improve the conditions of supply. When cholera returned again to London in 1853, Farr again analysed mortality rates by watersheds in London and was able to show that in an area where the water supply had been improved the death rate was lower than in adjacent areas.

Farr also developed a classification of causes of death, and made major contributions to occupational epidemiology, comparing mortality in specific occupations with that of the general population. Most famously in 1864, Farr highlighted the disproportionately high number of deaths among miners in Cornwall, showing that at each age the rate of mortality attributed to pulmonary diseases among miners was much higher than among males in the general population, concluding that the labour conditions inside mines contributed to these diseases. William Farr remains one of the major figures in the history of epidemiology.

Francis Galton (1822–1911) and Karl Pearson (1857–1936)

Increasingly, demographic practice was being influenced by modern statistics. The publication of Francis Galton's *Natural Inheritance* in 1889, and Karl Pearson's *The Scope and Concepts of Modern Science* in 1891 and *Mathematical Contributions to the Theory of Evolution* in 1893 are seen as the commencement of a new respect and awareness of statistical analysis. Galton and Pearson's work led to a new conviction that the analysis of statistical data would provide answers to many scientific questions. Data was now being collected in huge amounts, and statistical advances such as the correlation coefficient and other methods for measuring association, the invention of chi-square, and a growing emphasis on probable error formulae were laying the foundations of modern science. The Fisher–Tippett 'law of distribution' of 1928 heralded the era of big data science.

Sir Ronald Aylmer Fisher (1890–1962)

Sir Ronald Fisher was born in 1890, in London. At the age of 19 Fisher was awarded a scholarship to study mathematics at the University of Cambridge, graduating with a BA in astronomy. Once again we see the pervasive interest in astronomy amongst our theorists. Whilst at first these fields may appear divergent, the ultimate goal of both is an increased understanding of the unknown characteristics of our world, reducing large amounts of information into manageable data. Viewed in this light, the link between stars and people becomes clearer.

Fisher developed an interest in evolutionary theory during his student days, becoming a founder of the Cambridge University Eugenics Society. After leaving university Fisher taught mathematics and physics and was then appointed statistician for the Rothamsted Experimental Station, where he worked on plant-breeding experiments. In 1933 Fisher was selected as the Galton Professor of Eugenics at University College London, and from 1943 until 1957 worked as the Balfour Professor of Genetics at Cambridge.

Fisher's major innovation was his 'origination of the concept of analysis of variance' (ANOVA). 'Fisher's principal idea was to arrange an experiment as a set of partitioned sub experiments that differ from each other in one or more of the factors or treatments applied to them. By permitting differences in their outcomes to be attributed to the different factors or combinations of factors by means of statistical analysis, these sub experiments constituted a notable advance over the prevailing procedure of varying only one factor at a time in an experiment' (*Encyclopaedia Britannica*).

At the age of 60 Fisher was knighted, and four years later published *Statistical Methods and Scientific Inference*. Fisher's advances in mathematical probability highlight the development in 20th-century demography from the 18th century. Francis Bacon, whose endorsement of empiricism influenced the founding members of the Royal Society, understood that if one relies too closely on bald experience one will miss the forest and only see the individual trees. Both Petty and Graunt clearly foresaw that mathematical analysis could, to some extent, allow an observer to rise above individual cases and to see larger patterns. Two hundred years later this was realized by theorists such as Fisher and Tippett.

Leonard Henry Tippett (1902–1985)

Leonard Tippett was born in 1902, twelve years after Fisher. Tippett studied physics at Imperial College London. Next, he became a Master of Science in statistics, studying under Karl Pearson at Galton Laboratory, University College London, and under Fisher at Rothamsted. In 1928, Ronald Fisher and Leonard Tippett formulated the three types of limiting distributions for the maximum term of a random sample. Fisher and Tippett presented a theorem which can be considered as a founding stone of the extreme value theory. This theory deals with the study of the limiting behaviour of non-degenerate probability distributions of vectors of componentized maxima of random variables.

International Union for the Scientific Investigation of Population Problems (IUSIPP)

With the founding of the International Union for the Scientific Investigation of Population Problems in 1928, the field of demography moved away from a reliance on key figures, to draw more on a growing professional body of demographers; though as before, many had no formal training in demography itself. The first global population conference was held in Geneva in 1927, with an emphasis on the crucial nature of the population problems and their influence on social, economic, and political situations. At the end of the scientific meetings of the conference, it was decided that a permanent international organization should be set up to consider in a purely scientific spirit the problems of population. The IUSIPP was founded in Paris, with a predominant focus on Europe. It was reorganized in 1947 as the International Union for the Scientific Study of Population, extending its interest and expertise to less developed countries and the emerging economies.

By the early 20th century, demography was recognized as a separate field of study, with the first university courses being taught, key theorists recognized, and a clear set of methods and techniques developed. Among the key institutes are the Institut National d'Études Démographiques (INED), a French research institute specializing in demography and population studies, and the Max Planck Institute for Demographic Research (MPIDR), located in Rostock, Germany. The Population Reference Bureau (PRB), founded in 1929, is a private, non-profit organization which informs people around the world about population, health, and the environment for research or academic purposes.

The Western baby boom in the post-war years and the rapid population growth in the developing world highlighted the value of population forecasts. A paper by John Hajnal, 'The prospect for population forecasts', presented at the 1954 World Population Conference in Rome argued for greater flexibility and variety in techniques for projecting births. Hajnal was Professor of Statistics at the London School of Economics, and his most famous work was 'European marriage patterns in perspective', published in 1965, which identified a fundamental distinction between the marriage patterns of Western Europe and those of populations of Europe east of an imagined line connecting St Petersburg and Trieste—the Hajnal line.

There are now numerous well-respected and influential demographers working across the world. When members of the demography community were asked to name the most influential names of the 20th century three names topped the list: Ansley Johnson Coale, William Brass, and Jack Caldwell. These are all generally recognized as making a key and unique contribution to the discipline.

Ansley Johnson Coale (1917–2002)

Coale was one of America's foremost demographers, especially influential for his work on the demographic transition and leadership of the European Fertility Project. Coale was educated at Princeton and joined the faculty in 1947. He spent his entire academic career at the University's Office of Population Research, serving as director from 1959 to 1975. He was president of the Population Association of America in 1967–8 and president of the International Union for the Scientific Study of Population from 1977 to 1981.

Coale's first major influential work was *Population Growth and Economic Development in Low-Income Countries* (1958), which showed that slowing population growth could enhance economic development. This study was followed by *Regional Model Life Tables and Stable Populations* (1966). These model life tables both established new empirical regularities and proved invaluable in the development of later techniques for estimating mortality and fertility in populations with inaccurate or incomplete data. Along with William Brass, Coale pioneered the development and use of these techniques.

His major scientific contribution, however, was to the understanding of the demographic transition. Coale was the architect of the European Fertility Project, which examined the remarkable decline in marital fertility in Europe.

William Brass (1921–1999)

William Brass was one of Britain's most distinguished population scientists, creating a new and important strand of demography.

Bill Brass was born in Edinburgh in 1921 and studied at Edinburgh University from 1940 to 1943 and again, after war service, from 1946 to 1947. From 1948 to 1955 he was Statistician, and later Deputy Director, in the East African Statistical Department. There he worked on the East African Medical Survey and some of the early colonial censuses and it was during this time that he developed many of his ideas on the collection of demographic data and techniques for their analysis. The central problem that he addressed focused on the situation in developing countries where most births and deaths are not recorded, thus how can reliable estimates be made of death rates, birth rates, and trends in the size and structure of a population? Brass devised a series of ingenious answers to this question, demonstrating how child mortality levels and totals could be derived from simple questions to mothers on numbers of children born and still surviving; and how adult mortality could be estimated by asking people whether their father or mother had died.

From 1965 until his retirement in September 1988, Brass worked at the London School of Hygiene and Tropical Medicine. In 1974, with support from the then Overseas Development Administration, he created a Centre for Population Studies at the school and became its first director. In 1985 he was elected President of the International Union for the Scientific Study of Population, a post that spanned a term of four years.

John 'Jack' Caldwell (1928–2015)

Jack Caldwell's first academic appointment was as a Senior Research Fellow at the University of Ghana (1962–4), where he initiated a demographic studies unit and started field work on African population dynamics. This early experience began a lifelong interest in Africa. He returned to Australia in 1970 to become Head of the Department of Demography at the ANU, a position he would hold until 1988 when he moved to take up the Associate Directorship at the National Centre for Epidemiology and Population Health (NCEPH).

It was during his time on secondment as Regional Director for the Population Council and Professor of Demography at the University of Ibadan, Nigeria (1972–3) that Caldwell co-directed the Changing African Family Project. This used demographic and anthropological approaches to identify those transformations in African society which contributed to fertility decline. The subsequent *Manual for Surveys of Fertility and Family Planning* (which was written mostly by Caldwell and his wife Pat) played a pivotal role in the development of the World Fertility Survey (WFS).

As the enormous scale of the HIV/AIDS epidemic became clear in the late 1980s, Caldwell applied his knowledge of African family systems to understand what he termed 'sexual networking', working with academics in Uganda, Ghana, and Nigeria on the social context of the HIV/AIDS epidemic. In 1994, Caldwell became President of the IUSSP. The John C. Caldwell Chair in

Population, Health and Development was established in 1998 to honour his contribution; he is cited by the United Nations as 'one of the most influential and prolific scientists in the field of population...his work to frame the HIV/AIDS epidemic in Africa as a demographic, epidemiological and socio-cultural phenomenon is unparalleled'.

Theories and models in contemporary demography

The 19th and 20th centuries saw the development and consolidation of key concepts within demography. Important is statistical analysis and its various concepts such as index, rate, ratio, etc. Modern demographic data is voluminous and thus summary functions and indices, weighting, standardization, and comparison are all now essential components of demographic analysis. Formal demography deals with mathematical approaches to the treatment of deficient or non-existent population data; and methods dealing with uncertainty and credibility including simulation are now increasingly used. In particular new theories, assumptions, and methods to project future demographic trends are a key component of modern demographic techniques. Many of these are dealt with in Chapter 7, where we discuss the demographers' toolbox.

The discipline of demography, which started as a collection of ideas driven by an appetite for knowledge and scientific enquiry characteristic of the spirit of the 17th century, has matured into a formal discipline, supported by an international professional body, concerned both with the scientific understanding of population dynamics and their interaction with social, economic, and political factors. The sponsorship of the Royal Society over the first centuries of enquiry has been replaced by the IUSSP, though in 2012 the Royal Society again returned to the Population Question with its global report on *People and the Planet*.

Chapter 5
The drivers

The size, growth, density, distribution, and age structure or composition of a population is broadly dependent on three drivers: fertility (or numbers of births), mortality (or number of deaths), and migration (or number of moves in and out of that population). It is for this reason that most demographic analysis focuses on these measures.

The main measures of mortality are the crude death rate (CDR), the number of deaths to members of the population in the period divided by the total period person lives lived, and life expectancy, the average number of additional years a person would live under certain mortality conditions. The main measures of fertility in a population are the crude birth rate (CBR), which is the number of births per 1,000 population, and the total fertility rate (TFR), the number of live children born to the women of childbearing age within the population. Migration is different in that while mortality and fertility are typically studies within a closed population, migration introduces the notion of an open population—people do not just enter and leave via birth or death but also through entering and leaving the country or space under consideration. How demographers actually measure these drivers, and the data they use to do so, will be discussed in more detail in Chapter 7. Here we will explore the ideas behind our understanding of these drivers.

Mortality

In most cases mortality decline within a population occurs first at the younger ages, infants and children, and then progresses to adults, and finally pushes back average age of death of the oldest adults. In general terms improved nutrition, improved sanitation, the tackling of infectious diseases and finally of chronic disease, are the processes reducing mortality in a population.

As we have seen, in Europe it has been argued that 18th- and 19th-century trade, distribution, and transport systems increased the availability of food, public health initiatives enabled the safe storage and handling of food, and these contributed to better quality nutrition. Nineteenth- and 20th-century public health initiatives around sanitation enabled clean water, improved hygiene, and safe sewage disposal. The 20th-century introduction of penicillin and widespread vaccination programmes enabled the reduction in morbidity and mortality from infections and infectious diseases, and finally in the late 20th century pharmaceuticals and geriatric medicine made advances into tackling chronic disease and the morbidity of old age.

Another way of stating this is to say that *exogenous* mortality due to external causes such as infectious diseases has been replaced in advanced economies by *endogenous* mortality attributed to congenital defects or the ageing process, such as most cancers and cardio-vascular disease. We can explore this by considering mortality in different age groups within advanced economies. A new-born baby has a substantial risk of dying due to endogenous factors, such as congenital malformations. After the immediate post-partum period (or birth) exogenous risks such as infections and accidents become increasingly more important, and between the first and fifteenth year of life these are responsible for most deaths. After this endogenous factors start to take precedence again and deaths from heart disease and cancer slowly increase.

However, as the risk of succumbing to these in young and mid-adulthood is low, deaths from childhood onwards are pushed back into later life when the ageing body becomes particularly susceptible to these.

This helps to understand the rectangularization of the life curve in advanced economies, whereby deaths have been consistently pushed further and further back, so that most deaths there now occur after age 80 (see Figure 1). Currently life expectancy in advanced economies is 76 for men and 82 for women.

Similar factors are held responsible for the considerable mortality declines which occurred in the 20th and early 21st centuries in the less and least developed countries.

These, however, have impacted within a different context from the historical European case. In particular, the speed of diffusion and adoption has been faster, partly explained by the fact that while the European process emerged from within the countries

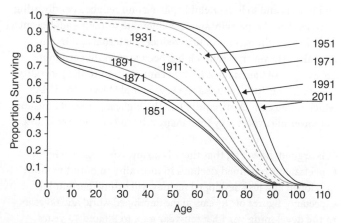

1. **Rectangularization of life curve for England. In 1850 few in England lived beyond 45, now over half will live to age 80.**

themselves over several centuries, many of the measures taken up in the developing world in the 20th century were introduced from advanced economies in a few decades. In addition, developing countries have benefited from the emergence of well-coordinated international programmes: for example, the work of the World Health Organization (WHO), established in 1948, in promoting global vaccination programmes; international famine relief programmes, such as the UN World Food Programme (WFP) and the Food and Agriculture Organization of the United Nations (FAO); and the emergence of the NGOs working to reduce poverty, famine, and morbidity—WaterAid, Oxfam, Save the Children, UNESCO.

In relation to both the historical mortality decline of Europe and the current falls in the less developed countries, these take place within a macro-level view that they are directly linked to economic development, industrialization and urbanization, increase in standards of living and GDP, and the related diffusion of education and health care. For example, increased levels of education within a population directly lead both to better outcomes for mothers and infants and to longer child-spacing and reduced childbearing in general, and especially among vulnerable women—adolescent and older mothers. This in turn reduces maternal and infant mortality. However, recently it has been argued that economic growth per se has made a limited contribution to the mortality decline in the 20th century. The key example here is the USA, which in the early 21st century had the highest per capita income, but lower life expectancy than many other advanced economies.

It is argued, however, that there is a slow convergence in life expectancy. Continued declines in mortality in both the more developed and less developed regions will extend current life expectancy figures of 78 years in the developed world and 68 years in the developing world, a ten-year gap, to 83 and 75 years respectively by the year 2050, thereby reducing the gap between developed and less developed regions by two years.

It is now recognized that the demographic transition has been accompanied by an epidemiological transition. This is characterized by a reduction in infectious and acute diseases and an increase in chronic and degenerative diseases. High death rates from infectious diseases are commonly associated with the poverty, poor diets, and limited infrastructure found in least developed countries. Now alongside these many such countries are also experiencing a rise in chronic and degenerative diseases. We can thus say that mortality across the life course from exogenous factors resulting from infectious diseases such as malaria and polio is now coinciding with an increased risk of death from endogenous factors such as cancer which are being exasperated through lifestyle changes, especially diet and smoking. The burden of infectious disease now lies alongside the burden of chronic disease in many countries of the South. Evidence from international epidemiologic research shows that health problems associated with wealthy and aged populations affect a wide and expanding swathe of world population. Over the next ten to fifteen years, people in every world region will suffer more death and disability from non-communicable diseases such as heart disease, cancer, and diabetes than from parasites and infectious diseases.

There is now interest in the question of life extension. Life expectancy and life extension are often confused but are two distinct concepts. In general terms life expectancy refers to the average years individuals can expect to live within a population. In technical terms life expectancy is the average number of additional years a person would live *if current mortality conditions applied*. This caveat is important and explains why current life expectancy for women in the UK is 82, and yet the Office for National Statistics (ONS) announced in 2014 that the first UK cohort of baby girls had been born with a life expectancy of 100. Indeed the life expectancy of babies born in many advanced economies in the early 21st century is probably around 103 (see Table 2). This is because across the lifetime of these baby girls the current death rates will change considerably, and they will

Table 2 Oldest age at which at least 50% of a birth cohort is still alive in eight countries

	2000	2001	2002	2003	2004	2005	2006	2007
Canada	102	102	103	103	103	104	104	104
Denmark	99	99	100	100	101	101	101	101
France	102	102	103	103	103	104	104	104
Germany	99	100	100	100	101	101	101	102
Italy	102	102	102	103	103	103	103	104
Japan	104	105	105	105	106	106	106	107
UK	100	101	101	101	102	102	103	103
USA	101	102	102	103	103	103	104	104

Data are ages in years. Baseline data were obtained from the Human Mortality Database and refer to the total population of the respective countries.

benefit from this. Most of their lives, therefore, they will not be living under the current mortality conditions. Increases in life expectancy are driven to a large extent by falls in mortality at younger ages, as more infants, children, and young people survive so the average life expectancy of the population is increased. In advanced economies, life expectancy has been increasing by two and a half years per decade for the past 150 years or six hours per day.

Life extension is the pushing back of maximum years a human population can reach. Humans have been designed to live long enough to reproduce and ensure the survival of their offspring. This is the 'essential life span'. But in most countries of the world most of us live well beyond this essential life span. In advanced economies, the greatest falls in mortality are now being experienced in later life, among the oldest old. So much so that life expectancy is beginning to bridge up against the concept of life extension. The drivers of life extension appear to be fourfold: healthy living, disease prevention and cure, age retardation or senescence prevention, and regenerative medicine. It has been argued that healthy living and disease prevention and cure can push most lives in the developed world to the century. Indeed centenarians in the

Box 3 Will humans ever live forever?

Some people assert that advances in science will eventually allow humans to live for 1,000 years or more. Others ask whether human biology will permit extreme gains in life extension. While few believe that there is a 'fixed limit to human age', few believe that we are immortal. Reality probably lies somewhere between these extremes. Possibly in the future we will be able to replace so much of our bodies that we would become a bionic creature that was completely replaced and able to live forever. The fundamental question then is biologically, socially, and philosophically—is that really still a human being?

UK are likely to increase from around 12,000 currently to half a million by the middle of the century and over 1 million by the end. Eight million alive in the UK are likely to reach a century, 127 million in Europe. However we shall probably need age retardation and regenerative medicine to achieve real life extension (Box 3).

Fertility

In terms of fertility rates, one-third of the world's countries are now at or below replacement level—crudely defined as a total fertility rate of 2.1. These are diverse, including Hong Kong, Poland, Germany, Barbados, Thailand, Vietnam, Mauritius, Iran, Chile, Tunisia, the USA, and Myanmar (see Table 3). A further

Table 3 Total fertility rate, 2012

Hong Kong	1.3
Germany	1.4
Vietnam	1.8
Iran	1.9
USA	1.9
Argentina	2.2
Venezuela	2.4
India	2.5
Pakistan	3.3
Zimbabwe	3.6
Afghanistan	5.1
Chad	6.4
Niger	7.6

fifty-eight are low medium—that is with a TFR of 2.1–3.0—these include Ireland, New Zealand, Indonesia, Argentina, Sri Lanka, Bangladesh, Mexico, Venezuela, Botswana, Egypt, Samoa, and India. Eighteen are at high medium 3.0–4.1—including Zimbabwe, Bolivia, and Pakistan. Forty-eight remain high—4.1 and above; most but not all are in sub-Saharan Africa, and most are classified by the UN as least developed countries.

The actual drivers of declines in childbearing have been long debated but broadly fall into three positions. One theory is that childbearing falls in response to a fall in infant mortality, in other words, increase in child survival rates reduces the number of births required to achieve the desired number of surviving children. It has been argued that fertility decline has never occurred in the absence of mortality decline, though there is some evidence that fertility decline did precede mortality decline in the USA and France. A second position is that the introduction of modern family planning methods has allowed women to choose the number of births they have. While some contraception has been used in many traditional and historical societies, modern forms of contraception allow more successful family planning. The third broad hypothesis is that fertility fall is driven by education. There is a strong association between those countries with a high level of educated women and those with below replacement fertility levels. Similarly, those countries with low rates of female education have high rates of childbearing. Educating girls, in particular, encourages later marriage and gives them access to the labour market, which reduces the number of births, but also and crucially it changes the 'mindset' of the women and their communities and enables them to recognize the range of alternative choices they can make. Indeed one of the greatest contemporary demographers, Jack Caldwell, identified 'ideational change' as the biggest factor in falling fertility. Recent developments in this area at the micro-level of decision making have drawn on psychological theories to help understand the role of individual psychological traits and how these may determine attitudes to childbearing and family size.

In 1950 Europe's total fertility rate was 2.5 children per reproductive woman; this had fallen to 1.5 by 2010. In Western Europe, all countries bar France are now below replacement level, and southern Mediterranean countries are at 1.2 and 1.3. In Asia, Singapore, Korea, and Hong Kong have now fallen to below 1.2. Indeed, some demographers have expressed concern that due to demographic inertia, a very low fertility rate could become irreversible.

The arguments over low fertility coalesce around three main concerns: couple replacement; young and midlife adult replacement; and environmental pressure. It is often argued that it is a natural desire for a couple—man and woman—to wish to replace themselves and that this is translated into the 'two-child norm'. While genetically each child having half the mother's and half the father's genes means that one child would suffice, it may be risk-averse behaviour, even in low-mortality societies, or the aim for one of each sex, or a sociological desire for a sibling for the first child. This is personal optimal fertility at the level of individuals and couples. Optimal fertility at the societal level is often discussed in the context of either national population replacement or labour market replacement and in more recent years in relation to earth's carrying capacity. At the national level replacement fertility is closely related to the percentage of reproductive women in the population. If in a population there is a high proportion of women of childbearing age then you need a lower child-bearing rate to achieve population replacement; if you have a low proportion of such women then you need a higher level of childbearing.

Some Asian and European countries may well be in a so-called 'low-fertility trap'. This arises through both demographic factors, the fact that fewer potential mothers in the future will result in fewer births, and sociological factors in that ideal family size for the younger generations is declining as a consequence of the lower childbearing they see in previous generations. Here it is argued that countries with very low childbearing rates of below 1.5 for more than one generation become adapted to childless or one-child families, and it is then very difficult to raise fertility again. Employment patterns change, child care and schools diminish, etc. This appears to be the case in China, for example. Here the one-child policy has been in place for thirty years, and we thus have a large number of one-child children who are now of childbearing age. Despite the fact that they are allowed two children, survey evidence suggests that many are choosing to have just one child themselves, because this is their own experience—they grew up in a society of single children.

Rapid population growth and high fertility threaten the well-being of individuals and communities in the poorest developing countries. While family planning/sexual and reproductive health programmes have made significant advances globally in helping women achieve the family size they desire, in some parts of the world, in particular sub-Saharan Africa, fertility decline is slowing or even stalling. In this region total fertility rates remain high at between four to seven births per woman. Considering the broad macro-factors (see Chapter 2), it is clear that low education, lack of family planning, and infant mortality all contribute to keeping fertility high in this region, though they are not the only factors.

Evidence suggests, for example, that continuing high rates of infant and child mortality are significant barriers to fertility decline in sub-Saharan Africa. This region has the highest level of child mortality, with an infant mortality rate of 64 deaths per 1,000 live births in 2012, some 2 million deaths, accounting for nearly half of all infant deaths globally. Similarly, there is a strong association between those countries with a high level of educated women, at least 60–80 per cent of the female population of reproductive age having completed at least junior secondary education, and those countries with below replacement fertility

Demography

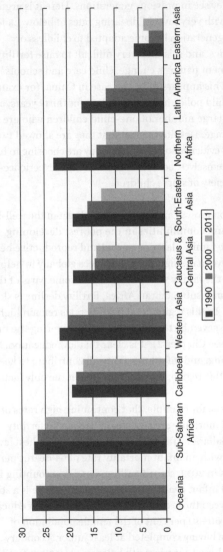

2. Percentage of women aged 15–49 who have an unmet need for family planning in 1990, 2000, and 2011.

Legend: 1990, 2000, 2011

Categories: Oceania, Sub-Saharan Africa, Caribbean, Western Asia, Caucasus & Central Asia, South-Eastern Asia, Northern Africa, Latin America, Eastern Asia levels. Similarly those countries with low female education rates of below 40 per cent of women of childbearing age having completed this level of education also have high TFRs. Girls' secondary education also dramatically affects fertility rates. A World Bank study found that for every four years of education that girls attain fertility rates drop by roughly one birth. Other research suggests that doubling the proportion of women with a secondary education reduced average fertility rates from 5.3 to 3.9 children per woman.

The unmet need for family planning is defined as the proportion of women aged 15–49, in a sexual partnership, wanting to postpone or avoid childbearing, but not using any method of contraception. Currently over 140 million women globally are in this position. As Figure 2 shows, the unmet need for family planning varies substantially with the highest levels of unmet need observed in Oceania and sub-Saharan Africa. However it is not straightforward to define levels of unmet need, as in some countries women may desire large families for cultural or social reasons, and thus contraceptive use is low, though the TFR is high. An example of this is Niger, where the TFR is 7.6, but the reported ideal family size is over 9.

Demographers working on fertility in this part of the world are well aware that the drivers of fertility fall are complex and research is also focused on family and social influences, cultural and religious factors, work, and other activities.

Migration

Migration has a potentially strong and long-lasting impact on population growth and structure through the interaction between the number of migrants, their relatively young age structure, and their higher fertility. Generally researchers distinguish between push and pull factors, arguing that migration flows arise from factors at both the origin and destination. The push-pull hypothesis assumes that at each end there are factors which promote and factors which retard movement, and that the balance between these factors determines the size and strength of the resultant population flow. For more than half a century the predominant global flow has been the immigration of human capital, in the form of migrant workers, from poor young countries in the South (southern hemisphere—Asia, Africa, and Latin America) to the rich old countries of the North—predominantly the USA and the European former colonial powers, such as Great Britain, France, and the Iberian countries of Spain and Portugal — in exchange for economic capital, both from national governments and in the form of individual remittances.

The first theories on international migration were developed some 250 years ago. A Swedish academic, Kryger, hypothesized in 1764 that the push factors of low wages and poor food distribution were forcing families to leave Sweden. Similar ideas were introduced in both France and England in the 19th century, suggesting that push-pull factors had to be accompanied by networks and communications between the regions or countries involved, and that a large flow in one direction would lead to a counter-flow in the other. Key here was the work of Ravenstein with his laws of migration, which are still used in some form by migration researchers today (Box 4).

Theoretical stances from economics, geography, and political science were introduced in the 20th century which emphasized the roles of enablers and barriers to migration—such as spatial and cultural distances, cost of movement, and government policies. Perspectives from sociology explored the relationship of power and prestige within a migration system, explaining some South–North–South moves in terms of low-status poor individuals moving to the North where savings are accumulated, enabling a return move to a higher-status position in the former country. Similar theories around feedback and return flows also emerged, proposing that a small group of migrants to a new region would

Box 4 Ravenstein's laws of migration

These were formulated by E. G. Ravenstein (1885) and state that:

1. Most migrants move only short distances.
2. Migration occurs in steps whereby the place of outmigrants is filled by inmigrants from more remote areas.
3. Each migration produces a movement in the opposite direction.
4. Long-range migrants usually move to urban areas.
5. Rural dwellers are more migratory than urban dwellers.
6. Females are more migratory over short distances; males are more migratory over long distances.
7. Most migrants are adults.
8. Large towns grow more by migration than by natural increase.
9. Migration increases with economic development and transport provision.
10. The major causes of migration are economic.

generate subsequent large flows, either through personal networks or through the establishment of professional bodies and agencies which provided assistance with moves. Demographers introduced ideas around assimilation of migrants into receiving countries and formalized the concepts of dependency burden and demographic potential to explain the move from the young South to the old North.

Nowadays it is recognized that push factors may be structural (macro) or individual (micro). At the macro-level rapid population growth and competition for resources may cause an out movement of people. Similarly war, famine, environmental crisis, persecution, and poverty are noted as individual motives. Pull factors are often loosely related to push factors and are difficult to distinguish. For example, the push factor of poverty in the South is reflected by the pull factor of the opportunity for wealth in the

North; lack of work in a rural area may push the migrant to move to an urban area where they are pulled by employment opportunities.

Intercontinental migration has long had an impact on population structures in both the advanced and less advanced economies. From the time of Columbus and the European discovery of the New World in the 15th century, most international migration flows originated in Europe and were directed to the Americas, and regions of the South in Asia and Africa. After the Second World War, migration from the South started to increase, as did migration within these regions (see Table 4). It is projected that the pull demand for immigrant labour in the North may be replaced by the push demand for better lives from the South. As a consequence the governments of the North may well introduce restrictions to reduce the current South–North flow. Others argue, however, that the predominant flows will increasingly be South–South and that countries in the North will begin to lose out on the skills and labour provided by workers from Asia, Africa, and Latin America. A key change over the past decade has been the increase in female migrants, particularly from Asia, as part of a growing health and social care immigrant labour group movement into the North.

Migration flows to and from sub-Saharan Africa have shown a change over the past half a century. Prior to 1960, the main flow was Europeans and Asians entering the region; this was reversed with the post-1960 decolonization whereby independence encouraged flows out of sub-Saharan Africa, mainly to Europe, for example the near 800,000 Portuguese inhabitants of sub-Saharan colonies who moved to Portugal in the 1970s, accompanied by expulsions, such as the British Asians from Uganda in 1972, and the Ethiopian Jews into Israel in the 1980s. The Middle East has long been attractive to foreign labour. However the origin of the migrants has changed from predominantly India, Iran, and Pakistan in the 1970s to include East and South-East Asia, in particular the Philippines and Indonesia. Alternatively,

Table 4 The net migration for world regions and selected countries. Net number of migrants, both sexes combined (thousands)

Major area, region, country	1950–1955	1955–1960	1960–1965	1965–1970	1970–1975	1975–1980	1980–1985	1985–1990	1990–1995	1995–2000	2000–2005	2005–2010
More developed regions	893	-607	2287	3728	6535	6532	6841	7907	11558	13923	17142	17412
Less developed regions	-893	607	-2287	-3728	-6535	-6532	-6841	-7907	-11558	-13923	-17142	-17412
Least developed countries	-502	-544	-851	-835	-4775	-4392	-6400	-3981	2738	-3467	-4640	-7457
Less developed regions, excluding least developed countries	-391	1151	-1436	-2892	-1760	-2140	-441	-3926	-14296	-10456	-12502	-9955
Less developed regions, excluding China	-875	471	-1739	-4043	-5456	-6667	-6637	-7668	-10732	-13758	-14965	-15601
Sub-Saharan Africa	-190	-132	-237	-81	-854	-1167	-1162	-1412	-450	-1137	-429	-184

(continued)

Demography

Table 4 Continued

Major area, region, country	1950–1955	1955–1960	1960–1965	1965–1970	1970–1975	1975–1980	1980–1985	1985–1990	1990–1995	1995–2000	2000–2005	2005–2010
ASIA	-242	1399	173	-57	-1789	-1404	-308	-2632	-7155	-6189	-8074	-9729
Eastern Asia	-530	108	-620	805	-1072	15	325	-432	-1096	-715	-1667	-1042
China	-166	-8	-1059	-13	-1113	-428	-258	-236	-824	-607	-2298	-1884
Southern Asia	-530	108	-620	805	-1072	15	325	-432	-1096	-715	-1667	-1042
India	-107	-4	-86	-246	2119	1131	483	45	-127	-443	-1923	-2978
EUROPE	-1273	-2995	521	-106	2125	2018	2164	3088	5487	4112	9373	9288
Eastern Europe	60	-1951	-1137	-360	-177	488	918	135	1222	1092	1036	2581

immigrants from South Asia have predominantly continued their association with Great Britain, though the moves to other Asian and European countries have also increased. Immigration from Indo-China, Korea, and the Philippines into the USA has been steady over the past decades, both due to conflict—a near 1.5 million being resettled in North America and Europe during and after the Korean, Cambodian, and Vietnamese conflicts, and through labour migration. As with Africa, until the 1950s South America was a receiver of predominantly European migrants, this reversing in the latter part of the 20th century, as those from the region moved to former European colonial powers and the USA. An interesting example of return migration is the migration of Brazilians and Peruvians of Japanese descent into Japan. This followed a decision by the Japanese government in the 1980s to allow overseas persons of Japanese descent to settle back in Japan.

The existence of migratory flows within rural areas and from rural to urban was theorized in the 1970s by Zelinksy, who argued that there were successive temporal phases of migration, first rural to rural, then rural to urban, then urban to urban. While this is seen as too simplistic to explain inter-country moves, the description tends to hold true in many countries. Of particular contemporary interest is rural–urban migration as this is a key contributor to urban growth. Here both push and pull factors are identified; population pressure in rural areas reducing access to natural resources such as food and shelter, or the introduction of new technologies removing agricultural jobs, provides the push. The pull comes from availability of education and medical facilities, higher incomes, and employment opportunities in the cities. Whatever the cause, rural outmigration to urban areas has undoubtedly contributed to the rapid growth in urban centres over the past centuries. It has been estimated, for example, that two-thirds of the near half a billion increase in the urban population of China over the past fifty years has been due to rural–urban migration. In other parts of the world, rural-to-rural migration is high. In South Africa a number of studies using data from rural demographic

Box 5 Why do women live longer than men?

In all societies once women have gone past reproduction, they tend to live much longer than male counterparts and it does seem that the female body is built more for longevity than the male body. For example, in terms of genetic make-up, women have two X-chromosomes, XX, and men only have one, XY. Thus if a woman has a failure on an X chromosome the second one can compensate, but a man does not have that advantage. There is also some interesting evidence around our hormonal systems. Oestrogen, the female hormone, protects against many of the diseases that affect the body, but the male hormone, testosterone, not only does not protect, it may even enhance morbidity and death. It also appears that the female immune system is stronger than the male immune system, and the male immune system does not seem to fight off either bacterial or viral infections as well as the female immune system.

surveillance sites (DSS) have documented an increasing trend of migration to other rural villages, semi-urban towns, and the rural perimeters of metropolitan areas, with evidence that over 40 per cent of the population has migrated from one district to another at some time during their life (Box 5).

Chapter 6
The demographic transition—centrepiece of demography

The 'demographic transition' is regarded as one of the centrepieces of demography. This is the continued fall in mortality and fertility rates whereby countries move from high death and birth rates to low death and birth rates. As we saw in Chapter 2, until the 18th century populations grew, stagnated and declined, and then grew again. Fertility and mortality responded to environmental and social changes—war, famine, abundance, dislocation. However, in the 18th century a new transition occurred, one which led to the immediate expansion of the population—as with the agricultural transition of the Neolithic period—but then to a steady decline of fertility leading to population decline and ageing. Commencing in Europe sometime after 1750, in Asia and Latin America during the 20th century, and with indications now that Africa will transition during the 21st century, this appears to be a fundamental break in the growth/decline/growth cycle that had occurred across human history until then.

Why the European demographic transition occurred when it did, where it did, and how it did is strongly debated, as is its counterpart in the South. However, as humans economically develop, mortality falls, population grows, fertility falls, and growth levels out or even declines. Demographic transition theory (or theories) can be divided into three broad components. The first part describes the changes over time in mortality and fertility. This part is generally based on clear data and is uncontested. The second component is most controversial as it attempts to construct causal models which might explain the timing, pace, and drivers of these changes. The third part is most uncertain as here demographers attempt to predict future changes especially for countries of the South.

The classic demographic transition is perceived as comprising four main stages (see Figure 3). In stage 1 populations experience high death rates from disease, famine, malnutrition, lack of clean water and sanitation; there is no impetus, or even the thought, to reduce fertility—these populations have high birth and death rates, and a relatively small but often fluctuating population size, for example England pre-1780 and current day Ethiopia. Stage 2 sees improvements in public heath, sanitation, clean water, and food, and mortality, especially infant and child mortality, falls. There are, however, still high fertility rates, resulting in a rapidly expanding population size—for example 19th-century England and current day Sudan. In stage 3 rapidly falling total fertility rates occur alongside low mortality rates. There is a still expanding but slowing population size such as in England in the early 20th century and Uruguay. Stage 4 sees low mortality and fertility, and a relatively stable, ageing population—current day UK and Canada, for example. During the late stages of the demographic transition, demographic inertia may set in whereby a well-below-replacement level of fertility becomes established over several cohorts. This would lead to a decline in population numbers were populations not maintained by inmigration. While many see this as the end stage of the classic demographic transition, some have suggested that it represents a second demographic transition.

It is argued that the transition brings a broad and profound change to human societies. Mortality decline leading to a greater likelihood of reaching adulthood and longer lives ensures a certain stability, people are able to plan for the future, to save and to

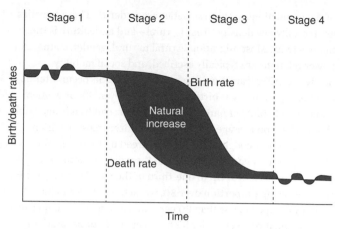

3. Demographic transition.

invest in both economic and human capital. The increase in population growth leads to migration and population density or urbanization, which in itself results in a more complex division of labour and systems of administration and governance. Family roles and relationships alter, and with fertility decline women are able to live lives that are more akin to men's. Demographically, populations move from having large numbers and proportions of young dependants to large numbers and proportions of old dependants. There is thus a change in dependency ratios, which are a measure of working age populations to dependent age populations, both old and young, and in support ratios, which measure working age to elderly dependants.

For example, a typical pre-transitional society will have life expectancies at birth of under 40 years, and women will spend most of their adult lives bearing children and will expect on average to have four to seven children, many of whom will die in infancy and childbirth. As a result there is a relatively high probability that the parent will outlive the child. Around 40 per cent of the populations in these societies are under 15. These societies are typically low density—that is, rural—and agriculture is the main activity. Most migration is rural to rural, gender, status, and power relations are typically ascribed, and social mobility negligible. After transition, the majority of deaths occur after 65, and life expectancies at birth are over 75 or even 80 for women, and the probability of parents outliving their children is negligible. Women bear on average two or fewer children, most of whom survive to adulthood, and having thus freed up their time for other activities, play a greater role in the wider economy and polity of the societies. Up to one-third of the population is over 60, with a growing proportion over 80, while those under 15 have typically dropped to less than 20 per cent. Now up to three-quarters of the population lives under high-density conditions in urban areas, and there is a merging of rural and urban lifestyles. More time is spent by all in education and a diverse range of occupations are now undertaken, mainly in the industrial and service sectors. Most migration is now rural to urban or urban to urban. Social mobility increases, and gender and power relations become more fluid.

Theorizing and re-theorizing the demographic transition

Early writing on the transition by Thompson in 1929 and Carr-Saunders in 1936 already identified the transition as a series of stages. However it was Notestein, writing in 1945, who is generally acknowledged to be the first theorist to try to concisely explain the theory of the demographic transition. He argued that urban industrial life stripped the family of many of its functions. The growing demand for skilled labour under industrialization and thus the need for education increased the costs of children and reduced their potential economic contribution via paid labour. Falling death rates were increasing the number of children who survived and this had to be supported. In response, births of new children began to decline. Kinglsey Davis, writing in 1963, developed this last point, arguing that falling death rates increased not only the number of surviving children but also of longer-lived adults. This put a strain on both households and communities. There were, he argued, three options to families: outmigration, delaying of marriage, and increasing birth control. In the 1970s the Princeton European Fertility Project, under the lead of Coale, led to the development of the Princeton Indices, and concluded that European fertility decline was driven more by cultural diffusion around accepted family size and reproductive behaviour than by economic development. This fits in well with later theorizing by Caldwell, who stressed the transmission of ideas as being key to fertility reduction in developing countries.

The demographic transition theory has, however, been questioned in relation to both Europe and developing countries. In terms of applicability to Europe it has been argued that it does not explain why countries varied in both their timing and progression. In addition the relationship between the timing and speed of mortality decline and those of the fall in fertility has been so variable that the theory does not appear to account for all the events which have happened. The socio-economic pattern in fertility development is also not accounted for; however, given the significant difference in rich and poor, it is unlikely that one theory could explain both situations. Finally, once fertility has fallen, it then appears to move up and down, not remain steady as the classical model suggests.

The second half of the 18th century witnessed the great European transition—mortality showed signs of decline and life expectancies started to increase. While there were still crises such as epidemics and famine there was a steady overall decline in the death rate. The gains in life expectancy as a result increased steadily in the 19th and 20th centuries. England, France, and Sweden, for example, gained less than a month of life expectancy per year between 1750 and 1850, rising to two months per year from 1850 and four to five months per year over the 20th century. Encouraged first by improvements in living standards and public health, and then by vaccinations and drug therapy, first infant and child mortality fell, followed by falls across the life course until old age. For example, a comparison of causes of death between Italy and England/Wales in the 100 years between 1850 and 1950 reveals that two-thirds of the gains in life expectancy from birth (LE) at this time were due to control of infectious, respiratory, and intestinal diseases. Two-thirds of the gains in LE occurred in those under 15, and only about 15 per cent from reducing deaths of those over 40.

In the early stages of the mortality transition, economic improvements thus appear to be key drivers, while as mortality decline progresses medical advances and changes in lifestyle and behaviour become more important. In the late stage of the transition, the link between economic development and mortality decline appears to be decoupled, as exemplified by comparing 21st-century Italy with the USA, where Italy has half the GDP of the USA, but a longer life expectancy at birth, 80 years compared to the USA's 77 years. This is explained by reference both to the large inequalities in the USA and to the fact that high economic development may lead to unhealthy lifestyles—low levels of exercise, increased consumption of unhealthy foods and alcohol, promoting obesity and chronic disease.

In terms of the fertility transition, decline in European fertility was gradual. The total fertility rate in Sweden and England and Wales, countries where statistics allow its estimation, was 4 and 5 respectively in 1750, reaching 3 in both countries by 1875, and falling below replacement by 1900. Here macro- and micro-factors appear to have interrelated and the process was complex and cannot be associated with one clear driver. It also varied considerably across the continent of Europe. Clearly social and economic development was also an important influence. Yet even here the relationship was not straightforward. For example, fertility fell earlier and faster in rural France than in its economically more developed industrial neighbour Britain. Demographers suggest that this was in part related to the differing ages of first marriage, which were early in eastern Europe and late in northern and western Europe, and the spread of birth control methods out from late 18th-century France across the rest of Europe during the following century. This was reflected in high levels of fertility in the east and low levels in the west, especially in France. Indeed it seems that cultural, religious, ethnic, and political affiliations were important factors as well. As the Belgian demographer Lesthaeghe pointed out, birth rates fell earlier in French-speaking rural Belgium than in the urban centres of Dutch-speaking Belgium.

While the transition in developing countries shows similarity to that experienced by European countries, there also are striking differences. The main factor has been the rapidity of the transition in the South. The European transition started from a lower level of fertility and mortality and was steady and slow. There was often only a short lag between mortality fall and fertility fall resulting in a steady increase in population of below 1 per cent per year. The less developed countries started from higher levels of mortality and fertility. These fell faster but with a longer lag between mortality fall and fertility fall and thus rapid population expansion reaching more than 2 per cent per year in recent years.

While in Europe and other advanced economies, the pace of change was dependent on new ideas and innovations, in sanitation and public health, and then in medicine, emerging and diffusing through society, in the less developed world these innovations have been transferred from the richer countries and diffused at tremendous speed. As a result mortality fell significantly in the latter half of the 20th century, and life expectancy increased by over one-third in just fifty years. While the desire to reduce disease and death is universal, the wish to reduce childbearing and thus fertility rates is more nuanced and complex. As a result, while mortality rates have fallen, built in demographic momentum plus social and cultural practices have reduced the equivalent rates in falls in childbearing—and populations have as a result expanded dramatically. It is argued that the Malthusian check on marriage in Europe which lowered the birth rate—low or never married populations—has not occurred in the countries of the South.

There is still, however, a significant difference between the populations of less developed countries of Asia and Latin America—who generally are reducing their fertility rates—and least developed countries—the majority of which are in sub-Saharan Africa—whose mortality is falling more slowly and whose fertility remains high.

In relation to developing countries there is even more questioning of the relevance of demographic transition theory. While both fertility and mortality rates are falling in many emerging economies, there are also examples of countries which are developing and yet levels of fertility remain high. Indeed it is argued by some that the high variations in countries' size, history, culture, geography, and religion are complicating the classical demographic transition seen in Europe.

However, many still argue that the demographic transition remains the central theory of modern demography, and that you cannot understand contemporary development unless you place the demographic transition at its centre. Indeed it is here that economists and demographers differ. Economists typically believe that the demographic transition is something which follows on from economic growth; demographers believe that it is a more complex process driven by socio-cultural as well as economic factors. Indeed some go as far as to suggest that the demographic transition's implications for the economy are greater than economic factors for the transition, and that the transition has played as important a role in the process of development as has economic growth.

Some demographers now argue that low-fertility countries are in the midst of a second demographic transition which is keeping fertility well below replacement. This may be due to technological advances and changes in the labour market which have altered the costs and rewards of marriage and child rearing. Others suggest it may be ideational changes which have accompanied our increased affluence, leading to a focus on individual autonomy and self-realization. In particular the evolutionary link between the sex drive and procreation has clearly been broken through the introduction of modern contraception, and now reproduction is merely a function of individual preferences and culturally determined norms.

Chapter 7
A demographer's toolbox

This chapter looks at the tools, models, methods, assumptions, and uncertainties within the practice of demography. In particular demographers need to know that they are really finding out the things they want to know and that their methods and sources of data are robust and are accurately answering their questions.

It was only in the 20th century that interest was shown in fertility, migration, and age structure, as well as mortality. The mathematics of a stable population was developed by Alfred Lotka in 1907, showing how if age-specific mortality and fertility remained constant, so a population would develop a predictable fixed age structure. The total fertility rate developed by a German demographer in the late 19th century started to gain popularity in the 1930s, and cohort fertility analysis only after the Second World War. Coale in the USA and Brass in the UK produced fertility models in the 1970s. The 1980s and 1990s saw an increasingly sophisticated adoption of mathematical models, needed to cope with the growing availability of demographic data. The Lee–Carter 1992 model for forecasting mortality, for example, introduced the ability to cope with random variability. The arrival of modern computing methods transformed the power of demographic analysis. Multivariate analysis, the statistical technique by which the relationship between several variables may be assessed, so as to measure the association between several independent and one dependent variable, became possible. Multi-state demography, the study of population movement between various different states, was developed out of traditional life tables. Rather than just birth and death being the process of loss and gain, so marriage allowed entry, divorce exit from the population of married people, for example. Probability, competing risks, and hazard functions all became part of the demographer's toolbox in the new millennium.

Measuring the main drivers: the data

It is said that demographic breadth comes from censuses, whereas demographic depth comes from surveys. There are four main sources of demographic data: census, registration records, surveys, and ethnographic material. Recently bio-markers have been added to the demographer's toolbox.

The modern census has been defined as the process of collecting, compiling, and publishing demographic, economic, and social data pertaining to all persons within a specific time and territory. Commenced originally for tax or military purposes, regular census collection did not occur until the late 18th/early 19th centuries with the USA beginning periodic censuses in 1790 and Britain and France in 1801. Today censuses are regularly carried out for over two-thirds of the world's population.

Registration systems of vital records have long been an essential source for demographers. Vital statistics are the data concerning vital events, which is defined as a change in an individual status leading to a change in the composition of the population. These include true vital events such as birth and death, and secondary vital events such as marriage, divorce, and migration. Vital registration is the official recording of such events, through birth and death certificates, and has long provided the basic information for demographic modelling. Parish records of birth, marriage, and death commenced in England in the early 16th century, and compulsory civil registration in Scandinavia in the 17th century. It was not until the 19th century that the rest of Europe and North America had similar comprehensive records.

Surveys contribute significantly to demographic analysis. As well as enabling the description of current demographic characteristics and, with longitudinal surveys, some sense of the progress of demographic change, surveys also have the ability to discover associations between demographic variables and events. Starting as early as the 19th century, Booth and Rowntree conducted surveys in England with a demographic component. The 20th century saw a burgeoning of surveys, such as the UK National Surveys of Health and Development and the US Growth of the American Family. These were joined in the later 20th century with panel surveys which reinterview the same population over time, such as the US National Fertility Survey, and longitudinal sample surveys, interviewing different but nationally representative sample populations, such as the UK General Household Survey, and the US Current Population Survey. The KAP surveys assessing Knowledge, Attitude, and Practice with regard to family planning were an important set of international surveys supported by the US Population Council established in the 1950s; though later somewhat discredited due to their stated hypothesis that the introduction of family planning measures alone was a simple and effective method of reducing fertility levels in developing countries.

Major national and international surveys such as the Demographic and Health Surveys (DHS), the World Fertility Surveys (WFS), and the Health and Retirement Surveys (HRS) are now vital to the understanding of fertility and mortality, and to a lesser extent migration. This is especially the case in the developing world, where censuses and vital registration systems are often lacking or incomplete. However, surveys may vary in their robustness, validity, and representation, and often only indicate population behaviour and characteristics at the national or regional level within a country.

It is only in recent years that demographers have come to recognize the rich demographic information available at the micro-level through ethnographic studies, participant observation methods, and interviews. These typically contribute material on family and households.

Quantifying migration is a complex task requiring the integration of different data sources. Migration analysis uses two different sources of data: statistics on the stock of migrants in a given place and statistics on the flow of immigrants and emigrants over a given time period. There are various difficulties with this. The lack of comparability between data sources restricts clear estimates of movement; many countries do not record simple cross-border movement with their neighbours, such as with the EU, or exclude these movements from national analysis. Estimates of migrants within a country require longitudinal data, and flow statistics of movement depend on sophisticated data collection systems. Such data is regarded as politically sensitive; in developed countries the magnitude is often ignored; in developing countries it may not even be collected. In addition, many of these systems are established for administrative rather than demographic purposes, and thus collect data which is inappropriate for demographic statistical analysis.

France provides an example of some of these incongruities. The French Office des Migrations Internationales (OMI) collects migration statistics. Both recent immigrants and those who have been in the country for some time are included under one heading. Similar irregularities occur in the US, which records immigrants granted the right of permanent residency on arrival with those who gain it after several years of living in the country. Neither Canada nor the US publishes emigrant statistics. Both Belgium and Germany record immigrants and emigrants as those attaining or rescinding permanent residency. And the Nordic countries apply different definitions to migrants to and from fellow Nordic countries, from those outside Scandinavia. Added to these complexities is the common decision by countries to group together other countries into subregions which are not comparable. For example, the People's Republic of China and Taiwan may be listed separately or together under 'China', South-East Asian countries may be listed individually or as SE Asia or even 'Other Asia' to distinguish them from China and South Asia. The Americas may be listed as North, South, and Central, or linked.

A major challenge faced by demographers is the lack of reliable, robust data. A series of methods have thus been established to 'estimate' demographic data from indirect sources—for example, estimating infant and child mortality from the number of surviving children against those ever born; or adult mortality from data on widows and orphans. Other techniques will relate one set of data to another to calculate a third, such as estimating fertility rates from parity rates. Formal models have been developed to estimate complete data from partial, including Brass's logit life table system and Coale–Trussell's fertility model.

Measuring the main drivers: the methods and models

Mortality is the process whereby deaths occur in a population. The statistical study of death is viewed as the origin of demography, and the study of mortality remains one of the principle foci of the discipline. The crude death rate (CDR) is the number of deaths to members of the population in the period divided by the total period person lives lived. If we take a period of time—say the first decade of the third millennium 2000–10—we can say that for each full year that a person is alive they contribute one person-year to the total period person-years lived or PPYL. We can count up person-years in years, days per year (1/365 person-years), hours (1/8,766 person-years), or even minutes and seconds. The CDR clearly reflects the age structure of a population, as the higher the proportion of older people in a population, the higher the CDR is likely to be.

Life expectancy is the average number of additional years a person would live under certain mortality conditions. Life expectancy at birth is based on mortality conditions at all ages. The range of values for life expectancy at birth ranges from 20 in poor historical conditions to around 80 in modern advanced countries.

Increases in life expectancy, which are calculated from the average of the population under consideration, should not be confused with increases in human longevity, which refer to the maximum years lived by individual human beings.

The life table (Box 6) is a detailed description of the mortality of a population given the probability of dying and various other statistics at each age (see Table 5). A complete life table is composed of the values of various functions for persons of each age, an abridged life table uses age groups.

Box 6 The history of the life table

The life table occurs in several chapters of this book. That reflects its importance historically and currently to demography.

Until the late 19th century the main focus of formal demography was the life table, which analysed and presented mortality data. Graunt's analysis of the London Bills of Mortality in 1662, Edmond Halley's life tables based on real deaths in the city of Breslau in 1693, Milne's 1815 formalization of the calculation and presentation of the life table, and William Farr's production of the decennial series of English life tables from 1841, all contributed to the modern day life table. The United Nations started to produce model life tables constructed from partial information using a mathematical formula in the 1950s, and the Princeton Group in the 1960s. One of the most famous model life tables was published by Coale and Demeny in 1966.

Table 5 Life tables

Age	Males			Females		
x	lx	qx	ex	lx	qx	ex
0	100000	0.005976	75.958	100000	0.004835	80.585
1	99402	0.000448	75.412	99516	0.000309	79.974
2	99358	0.000252	74.445	99486	0.000214	78.999
3	99333	0.000173	73.464	99464	0.000161	78.016
4	99316	0.000145	72.476	99448	0.000132	77.028
5	99301	0.000132	71.487	99435	0.000117	76.038
6	99288	0.000122	70.496	99424	0.000108	75.047
7	99276	0.000116	69.505	99413	0.000103	74.055
8	99264	0.000113	68.513	99403	9.92E-05	73.063
9	99253	0.000114	67.521	99393	9.81E-05	72.070
10	99242	0.000118	66.528	99383	9.84E-05	71.077
11	99230	0.000128	65.536	99373	9.96E-05	70.084
12	99217	0.000145	64.544	99363	0.000102	69.091
13	99203	0.00017	63.554	99353	0.000108	68.098
14	99186	0.00021	62.564	99343	0.000126	67.105
15	99165	0.000274	61.577	99330	0.00016	66.114
16	99138	0.000375	60.594	99314	0.000215	65.124
17	99101	0.000524	59.617	99293	0.000266	64.138
18	99049	0.000665	58.648	99266	0.000281	63.155
19	98983	0.00076	57.686	99239	0.000284	62.173
20	98908	0.000783	56.730	99210	0.000287	61.190

lx are the number of survivors to age x of 100,000 live births of the same sex for a given country who subsequently experience mortality similar to that of the population of that sex, in that country in 2000–2.

dx are the number dying between age x and $(x+1)$, described similarly to lx, that is $lx - lx+1$.

qx is the initial mortality rate between age x and $(x+1)$, that is, dx / lx.

ex is the average expectation of life, the average number of years that those aged x will live thereafter.

The basis of the life table is a set of probabilities of dying which gives the proportion of individuals alive at age x who die before reaching age $x+n$. Given this set of probabilities a second set of values is presented for the probability of survival from birth to each age. Life expectancy from birth or additional life expectancy from age x is also often given.

A life table may be built on complete empirical data, that is there is information for all ages on deaths and the population at risk of death. Often, however, life tables have to be constructed from partial information, using a mathematical formula. These are then termed model life tables. Model life tables are also used to supply standard assumptions used in population projections and to reconstruct rates from historical counts of births and deaths.

Fertility is the childbearing performance of individuals, couples, groups, or populations. It is sometimes confused with fecundity, the biological capacity to reproduce, which may or may not lead to childbearing. A main measure of fertility in a population is the crude birth rate (CBR), which is the number of births to members of the population in the period divided by the total period person lives lived. This is usually expressed as the number of births per 1,000 population over a year. The CDR clearly reflects the age and sex structure of a population, as populations with a large proportion of young women in it are likely to have a higher CBR than those with a low number.

The total fertility rate (TFR) is a second important measure. Generally described, TFR is the number of live children born to women of childbearing age. In technical terms the TFR of a population is the average number of children that would be born to a woman over her lifetime if she were to experience the exact current age-specific fertility rates across her lifetime, and if she were to survive to the end of her reproductive life.

The number of live births that a woman has is known as her parity, which is derived from the Latin *parens*, meaning parent. A woman at parity 1 has had one child, at parity 2, two children, and so on. A nulliparous has not borne a child. The parity of a birth cohort of women who have completed their childbearing can thus be calculated by adding up the parity of each woman and dividing by the number of women.

Tempo refers to the timing of births, quantum to the lifetime number of births. Recent falls in childbearing reflect a change in tempo—particularly women delaying the age at which they have their first birth, and the spacing of subsequent births, as well as in quantum—the actual number of births completed. Demographers also distinguish between spacing behaviour, when parents undertake behaviours such as contraception in order to space out their children, and stopping behaviours, when contraception or sterilization may be used to prevent any subsequent births. Proximate determinants of fertility are biological and behavioural factors which directly influence fertility, and through which social, economic, and other factors come to influence childbearing. The alternative term 'intermediate fertility variables' is also sometimes used. These include contraception and marriage, for example (Box 7).

Box 7 Bongaarts' decomposition

Bongaarts' decomposition quantifies the impact of the four main proximate determinants of fertility variation.

1. Proportion of women married
2. Contraceptive use and effectiveness
3. Induced abortion
4. Post-partum infecundability—or the period post-birth of non-susceptibility to conception.

These four may account for up to 96 per cent of fertility change in some populations.

The study of the frequency, dissolution, and characteristics of marriages or formal sexual unions within a population is termed 'nuptiality'. Nowadays these include consensual union—a stable union without recorded legal sanction, referred to as customary marriage, common law marriage, or companionate marriage. Increasingly all such sexual unions are termed conjugal unions. The close link between nuptiality and fertility makes it an important component of demographic analysis. Crude marriage rate refers to the number of marriages within a population; the age-specific rate allows more detailed analysis and may be represented through a Nuptiality Table.

Contraception is action taken by sexually active couples to prevent conception. This may be to cease, limit, or space out childbearing. Most societies use forms of contraception, including abstinence and breast feeding. Particular interest is on the unmet need for modern forms of contraception or family planning. This is defined as the proportion of women aged 15–49 in a sexual partnership wanting to postpone or avoid childbearing who are not using any method of contraception. As a population measure it must be recorded along with desired family size, which may be large or smaller than the current total fertility rate.

Migration studies distinguish between within country moves, which may be rural to urban, urban to urban, or rural to rural, and in advanced economies a small number of urban to rural moves, and international migration which crosses country and regional boundaries. Some researchers argue that due to the fragmentary nature of the available statistics and impermanence of trends, there is little value in developing complex statistical models of migration.

The basic calculation on migration is for the immigration rate:

$$IR = I / P \times k$$

where I is number of migrants, P is the population of the country or designated area, k is a constant, often 1,000.

For outmigration:

$$OR = O / P \times k$$

and the rate of net migration is:

$$NR = I - O / P \times k.$$

Methodologically simple matrices are used to project such moves, while more complex models such as random walks, which use the mathematics of Brownian Motion, enable the demonstration of migration patterns. It is further possible to combine a random walk model for dispersion with a logistic model for growth. When these are combined population growth is seen to respond to density, and we typically see large populations in the centre of an area reduce their growth, while dispersed peripheral populations continue to increase. One such application of this, for example, modelled the movement of people following the Neolithic transition in Europe.

Considerable movement to urban areas over the past few centuries has led to the growth of large urban agglomerations and these

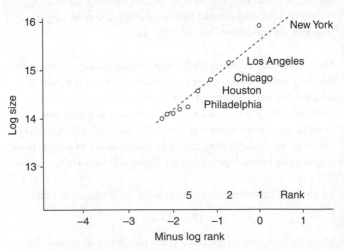

4. **Rank-size plot for US cities, 2010.**

may be studied using rank-size plotting. These are useful tools for identifying laws determining certain characteristics of cities, such as size. Figure 4 ranks the most populous cities in the USA, plotting minus the logarithm of the rank on the horizontal axis and the logarithm of the population count on the vertical axis. This is a power-law distribution where there are a few sizes much larger than the rest, which account for a large share of the total size. In this case a small proportion of cities accounts for a high percentage of all US urban residents. Such power laws are found in many other areas, including astronomy, in terms of masses in each galaxy, and economics where a few people own a large proportion of all wealth.

Demographers are also interested in the interrelationships between the main drivers; for example, the relationship between migration and fertility rates. Sex-selective migration will tend to separate men and women, reducing opportunities for childbearing in both the host and sending area. Women's childbearing may be disrupted by their own migration, though there is some evidence that fertility increases among recently immigrant women who take the opportunity to have children in the light of new opportunities for health, welfare, and education within the host area.

Chapter 8
Population pyramids and projections

A key concept within demography is the population pyramid. The age pyramid comprises a pair of bar graphs joined in the centre and traditionally resembling an Egyptian pyramid. The vertical axis records age, with young at the base and old at the top, and the bars coming off the axis to the right represent females and to the left males. The age pyramid thus represents the distribution of a population by age and sex (see Figure 5). Many modern age pyramids now resemble either a skyscraper or even a vase, as their populations have reduced their childbearing and increased their life expectancies.

Population change is expressed in the balancing equation. It may be formulated as

$$P_2 = P_1 + B - D + I - E$$

where P_2 and P_1 are population size at two different dates, B is births, D is deaths, I is inmigrants, and E is outmigrants.

While this equation may be used for countries or regions, the world population is a closed population, entering by birth and leaving by death—with currently no migration on or off the planet. The equation for a closed population is:

$$P(t+n) = P(t) + B(t) - D(t)$$

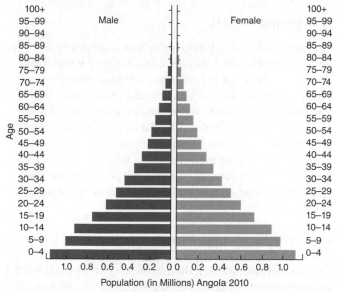

5. Population pyramid, Angola 2010.

Where $P(t)$ is the size of the population at time t, n is the length of a time period, $B(t)$ is births at time t, and $D(t)$ is deaths at time t.

Some demographers prefer to use K to denote population as P can be confused with the notation for probability. So you may see these equations stated as

$$K_2 = K_1 + B - D + I - E$$
$$K(t+n) = K(t) + B(t) - D(t)$$

The balancing equation for the change in world population from 2013 to 2014 is

$$P(2013) + B(2013) - D(2013) = P(2014)$$
$$6{,}851 + 140 - 57 = 6{,}934$$

77

Age, period, cohort

The demographic behaviour of individuals is affected by their age, the time period in which they are living, and their shared cohort experience. These age-period-cohort effects are central to demographic analysis. For example while dentists might notice a decline in dental health with age (an age effect), they may also notice a significant reduction in dental decay in everyone born after the 1960s due to the addition of fluoride in drinking water, which protects against tooth decay (a cohort effect), and a recent improvement of all patients regardless of age or birth year due to new dental techniques now available in their practice (a period or time effect).

Complex models are now used by demographers to tackle these interactions. These include fertility measures such as the net reproduction ratio, which is the number of newborn daughters per prospective mother who may or may not survive to and through childbearing, the cohort age-specific fertility rate, which is the number of children borne by women in the cohort between the ages x and $x+n$ per person-year lived, and period age-specific fertility rate, which substitutes the cohort person-years lived above with the count of babies born in the period under question.

One of the first of these was the Coale–Trussell fertility model developed in the 1970s, which is still widely used to detect the use of parity-specific birth control, in other words birth control in relation to the number of children already born to a mother. This is an example of a model which works well with historical data, but appears to have less relevance for the complexity of modern contraceptive decisions. For example, the model assumes that women have higher parity, or a higher number of children, as they get older. However, in contemporary advanced economies, such as North America or Europe, where we see a significant delaying of marriage and first childbirth by many women, we find high use of contraception, low parity but high fertility for women over 35. The emphasis for those studying fertility in these modern societies has been to focus not only on number of children in relation to contraceptive use, but also child-spacing as a form of family limitation.

In terms of mortality, the Lexis diagram represents both the life lines to death for individuals and for specific cohorts. We can also introduce measures of survival and probabilities of dying as a function of age for the cohort in question. We can also introduce growth rates and hazard rates—hazard rates measuring the chance of death occurring at each age or time period. One of the most famous of these formulae is the Gompertz model (see Chapter 4) which models the hazard function—or probability of dying—as a person ages. It was first described by the English actuary Benjamin Gompertz in 1825 to provide a model for the age-specific mortality rates he was observing. Again, modern complex mortality modelling is now undertaken. For example, the Lee–Carter model includes age-specific death rates and introduces random variability, treating the parameter of time as a time series, incorporating past fluctuations as indicators of the range of uncertainty about the future.

Age structure

It has been known for a long time that the demographic drivers of fertility, mortality, and migration will affect the age distribution of a population. In 1760 Euler developed the concept of the stable population. This idea was explored fully in 1907 by Alfred Lotka. Both identified the fact that if mortality and fertility remain constant for any length of time within a closed population, that is one without in- or outmigration, then a fixed age structure will arise, which is independent of the initial age structure. A stable population in terms of its age structure may be increasing or decreasing all the while its age structure remains fixed. If, however, there is no growth or decline, this is termed a stationary population.

We may explore how the three drivers independently affect age structure. A change in the level of childbearing, for example, will affect the youngest age groups, but will then work its way through to affect older ages as well. Falling fertility narrows the base of the population pyramid as births fall. A baby boom followed by a baby bust may create an early bulge which is clear within the pyramid until the baby boom cohort reaches very old age. The pyramid for the UK in the 20th century clearly shows the 1946 baby boom and then the slow decline until 1957 when births slowly started increasing, culminating in the UK's mini baby boom in the early 1960s (see Figure 6). As we move through the subsequent decades in the figure we can see the baby boom affecting the number of those of young working age in the 1970s and 1980s, and approaching retirement ages in the 2020s. The pyramid will also be affected by mortality rates as a decrease in lifetime death

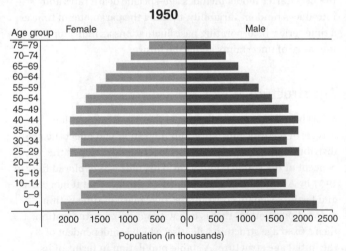

6. UK population pyramid, 1950.

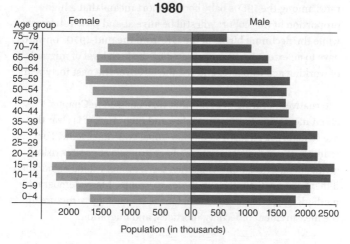

1980

Age group | Female | Male

75–79
70–74
65–69
60–64
55–59
50–54
45–49
40–44
35–39
30–34
25–29
20–24
15–19
10–14
5–9
0–4

2000 1500 1000 500 0|0 500 1000 1500 2000 2500

Population (in thousands)

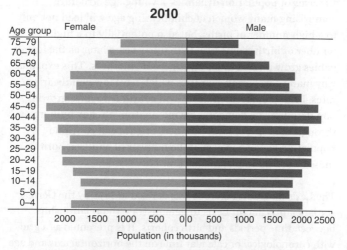

2010

Age group | Female | Male

75–79
70–74
65–69
60–64
55–59
50–54
45–49
40–44
35–39
30–34
25–29
20–24
15–19
10–14
5–9
0–4

2000 1500 1000 500 0|0 500 1000 1500 2000 2500

Population (in thousands)

6. (continued) UK population pyramids, 1980 and 2010.

rates among the 1960s baby boom cohort means that a high proportion of this cohort will still be alive at and post-retirement, while the declining births in the UK from the mid-1970s onwards have to an extent been compensated by the high level of migrants of working age who have entered the UK over the past forty years.

Alternatively, bearing in mind what we discussed in Chapter 5 about measuring fertility, mortality, and migration, it is clear that age structure itself has a significant impact on vital events. For example, if a high proportion of an age group is at greater risk of giving birth, dying, or moving, then these events will be higher than if there are small numbers in these age groups. Many demographic methods thus attempt to control for the effect of age structure in the measurement of fertility, mortality, and migration.

In terms of population dynamics, a young age structure comprising many women of childbearing age will lead not only to a high number of births, but also potentially to a high number of births some twenty to thirty years later as the female babies grow up and themselves become mothers. This explains why many developing countries which have low childbearing rates, below replacement level, will continue to have growing populations. The demographic momentum already built up through the birth of large numbers of girls will continue population expansion even if the number of children born to these future mothers remains low.

The Lexis diagram (Figure 7) was devised in 1875 by the German statistician Wilhelm Lexis to demonstrate the relationship between time periods and birth cohorts. It is presented as a grid with chronological or calendar time on the horizontal axis and age on the vertical, with diagonal lines running at a 45-degree angle up from the horizontal axis separating each cohort. Originally these lines actually ran downwards. Each line represents one person starting at the person's date of birth and age at birth (0). The lines go up at 45 degrees because the slope then equals 1,

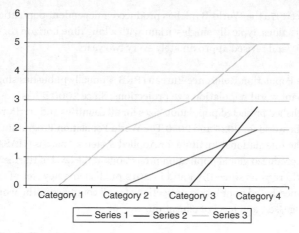

7. Lexis diagram.

and people age one year in every one calendar year. Each life line continues up until the age of the person's death is reached. By drawing a line at a specific time point the number of lives crossed equals the number alive at that time point and thus the total population number.

Population projections

The first modern global population projection was carried out in 1945 by Notestein of the Princeton Office of Population Research, using the cohort component method which explicitly considered the age and sex structure of the population.

Since 1958 the UN has published sets of estimates and projections for all countries since 1958. Before 1978 these projections were revised approximately every five years, and every two years since then. Recent UN assessments have a time horizon to 2050. At irregular intervals the UN World Population Prospects Series also publishes long-term population projections with time horizons from 2150 to 2300.

Since 1978 the World Bank has produced independent population projections, typically single variant with a long time horizon to 2150, and revised approximately every two years.

The Population Reference Bureau (PRB) annually publishes single variant world population size projections. Since 2000 it has published projected population sizes for all countries and territories of the world for 2025 and 2050.The World Population Programme of the International Institute for Applied Systems Analysis (IIASA) has produced global population projections at the level of thirteen world regions since 1994 and in 2012 published a new set of science-based population projections for all countries in the world by age, sex, and level of education.

Projection methods

Demographic projections aim to foresee population futures. These are based on assumptions about future vital statistics and on formulae to execute the calculations. There is a distinction between a projection and a forecast. Forecasts entail an element of prediction. Basic population projections focus on sex and age as the main divisions of a population. The main tools for projecting a population forward by these variables are tables called Leslie matrices after P. J. Leslie, who published a description of them in 1945. Leslie matrices are transition models which combine the effects of fertility and mortality to produce population change. The states correspond to age groups, and the process of transition is surviving and giving birth. The population is projected forward one step at a time.

The most widely used methodology for projections is component methods. In these each of the components of change—births, deaths, migration—is estimated. If each age group is also estimated cohort-component methods are used. More recently a variety of sophisticated multi-state models have been developed to make population predictions more robust. However, no matter how sophisticated the models become, they are still reliant on assumptions about future fertility, mortality, and migration. It is widely recognized that while the statistical models are now highly sophisticated, the theoretical basis of the understanding of demographic dynamics still requires greater predictive power.

The Leslie matrix is a table with rows and columns showing the expected number of individuals who start in the age group with the label on the column, and move diagonally through to the age group with the label on the row. The first row contains factors which reflect the level of fertility and survival; the principal subdiagonal contains survivorship ratios reflecting the chances of survival from one age group to another. Before data is fed into the matrix, logical zeros are inserted. For example, in Table 6 there will be no babies born to those age 0–5 so the element is 0. More complex versions of the simple Leslie matrix involve continuous age and time. Projection in continuous time is called population renewal and involves the notion that past babies are current mothers who will provide future babies (Box 8). The survival component in such complex models involves multi-state tables which include not just alive and dead but also states of illness and disability. Individuals thus enter, exit, and re-enter and re-exit certain states.

Table 6 Leslie matrix

	0 to 5	5 to 10	10 to 15	15 to 20	20 to 25
0 to 5	kids	kids	kids	kids	kids
5 to 10	survivors	0	0	0	0
10 to 15	0	survivors	0	0	0
15 to 20	0	0	survivors	0	0
20 to 25	0	0	0	survivors	0

Box 8 Renewal equation

'The decisions each of us, and the rest of humans like us, make about marriage, parenthood, and survival promoting behaviours will create the elements of the Leslie matrices of the future, write the scripts for the march of the cohorts up the world's Lexis diagram, and empower the Renewal Equation to do its work' (K. W. Wachter).

The renewal of a population occurs as newly born individuals replace those who have recently died. With current longevity rates it takes just over one century for the world population to be completely renewed.

The process may be expressed by the renewal equation:

$$B(t) = beta/alpha \; B \, (t-a) \; l(a) \; m(a) \; da + G(t)$$

This states that births at time t, $B(t)$, are determined by the summation from the lower and upper limits of the reproductive ages *alpha to beta* of the births a years which have been previously multiplied by the probability of these individuals surviving $l(a)$ and the probability of them giving birth $m(a)$ in the interval from a to $a + da$. In addition births already born to women need to be counted $G(t)$.

Chapter 9
Sub-disciplines arise

While most of the social science disciplines deal with people, some have developed a specific interest in demographic analysis and demographic theories, and these have been formalized into sub-disciplines of demography. In many cases they represent a merging of an area within the main discipline with demography. While many of the following can be recognized as distinct sub-disciplines, often with their own professional organizations and/or academic journal, it may also be argued that the divisions are imposed and even arbitrary. Studies in spatial demography, social demography, and population studies are often hard to distinguish; new complexities in bio-demography and genetics increasingly need the sophisticated modelling found in mathematical demography; and family behaviours such as household formation, marriage, divorce, and intergenerational transfers explored by economic demographers are sometimes indistinguishable from similar studies in family demography. In many cases it is a matter of where you publish, which society you belong to, and which annual meeting you attend, which places an academic's work within the sub-discipline. Despite these caveats, the general discipline of demography has been greatly enhanced by these new initiatives and forays into new methodological and theoretical territories which have occurred over the past few decades.

Anthropological demography

Anthropological demography uses anthropological theory and methods to provide a better understanding of demographic phenomena. It reflects a merger between social anthropology and demography, and while technically it is restricted to demographic studies of fertility, mortality, and migration in small human communities, in practice it addresses demographic processes in general. The intersection of two disciplines with contrasting methodologies is viewed as a positive interaction, combining interest in the dynamic forces defining population size and structure and their variation across time and space, with anthropology's focus on the social organization shaping the production and reproduction of human populations. The approach combines quantitative and qualitative methodologies applied to case studies, drawing both on ethnographic fieldwork and participant observation and on the interpretative reading of secondary data and historical material.

Academic papers defined as anthropological demography have appeared in demographic and anthropological journals since the 1980s, and Anthropological Demography sessions have been held since the 1990s in professional population meetings. Indeed the author of this VSI was faced with a choice at the 1995 Population Association of America meeting in San Francisco between attending anthropological demography sessions and demographic anthropology sessions held in opposing rooms along the same corridor, the first championed by demographers interested in anthropology, the second by anthropologists interested in demography.

Perspectives from anthropological demography provided important input into the European Fertility Project, bringing an understanding of the importance of cultural settings on fertility decline which was independent of socio-economic factors, and incorporating aspects of cultural and ideational change into the demographic transition theory.

Bio-demography

Bio-demography may be seen as a convergence of demography, evolutionary biology, and genetics. It typically involves the collection and modelling of biological indicators in conjunction with sample surveys and longitudinal studies. It is argued that conventional demographic data combined with genotype data will elucidate gene–environment interactions. For example, human population samples with sufficient representation among the oldest old should allow the identification of alleles concentrated among centenarians. Similarly, existing understanding about the inheritability of components of mortality risk and survival in terms of age-specific gradients will be greatly enhanced through mathematical formulae describing genetic influences shaped by evolution.

The development of bio-demography was directly encouraged by the Behavioral and Social Research Division of the US National Institute on Aging (NIA) under the leadership of Richard Suzman. In particular the 1997 volume *Between Zeus and the Salmon* is a landmark collection of early work in this area. Parallel work on the bio-demography of fertility and family is reflected in *Offspring* published in 2003, sponsored by the US National Institute of Child Health and Human Development.

Researchers argue that novel research in bio-demography has challenged classical formulations of the evolutionary theory of longevity, both through experimental and observational data and through mathematical and theoretical developments. Demographic perspectives have influenced research strategies for those biologists who have come to recognize the value of large population studies for generating life table estimates, along with the need for comparative formal modelling. Demographers introduced to the evolutionary theory of longevity have developed collaborations with anthropologists to rethink assumptions about the evolutionary environment in which genetic and biological determinants of age-specific vital rates have been shaped. Without doubt the coming role of genome science promises further transformations and challenges in this new sub-discipline.

Economic demography or population economics

Economic demography, demographic economics, or population economics may be defined as a branch of demographic research which addresses the relationship between population and economics. It is the application of economic analysis to the study of human populations, including size, growth, density, distribution, and vital statistics. While many see it as complementing labour economics, researchers within this sub-discipline also consider broad issues such as population growth and economic development, the economic consequences of ageing populations with their changing dependency ratios, and the importance of economic factors in determining rates of fertility, mortality, and migration within populations. Micro-level topics examine individual, household, or family behaviour, including household formation, marriage, divorce, fertility choices, education, labour supply, migration, health, risky behaviour, and ageing. Macro-level investigations may address such issues as population and economic growth, the impact of population on the distribution of income and wealth, population policy, savings and pensions, social security, housing, and health care.

Bernard van Praag was the founding president of the European Society for Population Economics (ESPE), in 1986, which was created in order to consider theoretical and applied research focusing on the role played by human capital and demographic variables in economics. He was also co-editor of the *Journal for Population Economics* and the *Journal of Health Economics*, an international quarterly that publishes original theoretical and applied research in all areas of population economics.

Family demography

The main concern of family demographers is the family and household, with a focus on kin living in co-resident groups. The sub-discipline aims to place sociocultural research at the centre of population dynamics, recognizing that human societies control reproduction, and that an understanding of childhood, marital and parent–child relations, and the dynamics of co-residence are of importance. It is thus argued that three dimensions characterize the family. First is the conjugal, the formation and dissolution of marital unions. Second is the consanguineal, the relationship between parents and children. Third is the residential, with the simplest pattern being the nuclear family—a combination of conjugal and consanguineal, or parents and children, and a more complex arrangement of households comprising groups, or kin living together, termed co-residence.

The IUSSP established a Scientific Committee on Family Demography and the Life Cycle in 1982 with a mandate to promote research in the area. Some see this as the formal beginning of the sub-discipline. At that time the main areas of research focused on measurement and estimation of household composition and family structures, the family life cycle, kin models, multi-state life tables, and household projection. Today family demography draws upon large individual-level census data suitable for comparative study of family and household composition, and a diverse range of macro- and micro-level research topics are included in the approach ranging from multi-generational households, children and media use, to 'grey divorce'.

Historical demography

Historical demography is defined as the study of the size and structure of past populations, the components of population change—fertility, mortality, and migration—and the factors that influenced them. Technically it refers to all past populations; however, the study of prehistorical populations more generally falls under the sub-discipline of palaeodemography.

It is the type of source material which gives the sub-discipline its particular challenge and uniqueness within demography. Generally unable to work with census and vital statistics, historical demography relies on sources such as parish records and nominative listings drawn up for reasons other than the enumeration of the population. Parish registers, for example, do not collect births and deaths, but record baptisms and burials; historical listings were for tax purposes or military service.

Consequently, historical demographers have developed their own special methodologies. Principal of these is family reconstitution, a form of record linkage which reorganizes the information in parish registers into family histories enabling standard demographic measures to be calculated. Developed in France in the 1950s, the researcher locates information pertaining to one couple-union or marriage such as date of marriage, dates of birth and death of spouses and of children, etc. In this manner it is possible to reconstruct entire extended families (see Figure 8). Some demographers restrict the term *historical demography* to this micro-demographic approach.

It is widely recognized that the French method of family reconstitution using parish registers owes much to the economic historian Pierre Goubert and the formal demographer Louis Henry. Henry in particular wanted to determine levels and schedules of what he called 'natural fertility', before deliberate control of childbearing within marriage came to be practised. This has been seen as an important moment in the history of population research as family reconstitution made it possible for historians and demographers to work together to undertake cohort analyses.

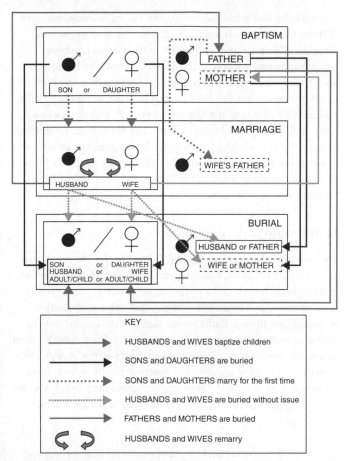

8. Example of a family reconstitution form.

The first official organization of historical demographers was the International Commission of Historical Demography (ICHD), founded in 1960. The Cambridge Group for the History of Population and Social Structure was founded in 1964 and is regarded as making discipline-transforming contributions to social science history. These include work on historical

93

demography and household structure, on the interdependence of these elements with welfare systems, and on occupational structure. The unique contribution of the Group combines demography and economic and social history. The European Society of Historical Demography was launched in 2014 supported by the Société de Démographie Historique (SDH), the Asociación de Demografía Histórica (ADEH), and the Società Italiana di Demografia Storica (SIDeS). The Society was established to foster the cooperation between scholars engaged or interested in historical demography studies in Europe, and stimulate interest in population matters within the European Union scientific programmes, agencies, and governments.

Mathematical demography

Mathematical demography may be defined as the presentation of demographic variables, their analysis, and interrelationships in mathematical terms. Lotka's work on the mathematics of stable populations is seen by some as the greatest single contribution to population theory. Lotka's work laid out the importance of momentum for future population growth. In other words the effect of a young age structure shapes the level and pattern of population growth until a stable population is reached. Keyfitz is seen as an important successor to the great mathematical demographer as he revealed the complex mathematical interaction between data, models, and theory.

One of the most influential pieces of mathematical demography remains the classic 1925 article 'On the True Rate of Natural Increase'. Here Lotka and Louis Dublin showed that the surplus of births over deaths in the resident American population was an artefact of a disproportionately large number of men and women in the peak ages for reproduction. The age distribution was itself the result of high rates of immigration. If the population of the United States were 'stable'—closed to migration in or out and subject to its current schedule of age-specific birth and death rates—then it would settle down to an unchanging age distribution and a characteristic low rate of increase. Lotka cautioned that Americans ought to be concerned about a declining population.

Nathan Keyfitz (1913–2010) made fundamental and highly influential contributions to demography over a long and productive career. His work was characterized by an elegance of approach and a depth of insight that came from a deep recognition of the interplay among models, data, and interpretation. A symposium, marking the 100th anniversary of his birth, will bring together a diverse set of scientists studying, to use Keyfitz's term, the mathematics of population. The main goal of the symposium is to serve as a forum for presentation of ongoing research on the mathematics of population. The programme will encompass research on human and non-human populations, and both theoretical and applied research.

Palaeodemography

Palaeodemography focuses on studies of the prehistoric patterns of human population growth and structure, including life expectancy, mortality rates at different ages, and general health and well-being indicators. Closely related to archaeology and physical anthropology, it relies on non-written sources including human and archaeological remains. Scholars describe their discipline as an estimation of the prehistoric population rather than an exact science. Burial grounds are rarely representative of the population as a whole, particularly as in many cases extended families, status groups, or age groups were all buried separately. In addition cause of death—warfare, accident, or disease—often remains the most identifiable marker on the skeleton, obscuring other diseases or signs of general good health.

Two areas of particular interest are the estimation of age and of disease and cause of death. The study of diseases in past populations is called palaeopathology. Age estimation comes from individual skeletons based on the most reliable markers of age, such as dental development and closure of joint connections. The discipline has now compiled a large human skeletal database against which individual measurements may be compared. Diet, health, and climate can significantly affect such measurements, making the determination of adult ages very difficult. While some diseases can be identified from individual skeletons by dental or bony lesions which indicate slowness of growth relating to biological stress, such as malnutrition, many diseases do not leave markers on bone, or only appear after the disease has reached an extremely advanced stage. Damage to the skeleton may be due to accidents or battles, and adverse working conditions also leave their mark on the bone.

However, new methodological advances are showing promising results. For example, the identification of microbial DNA in human bone has been used to recognize the presence of pathogens indicating the presence of disease. Similarly, analysis of stable isotopes in human bone have enabled researchers to identify the locations where an individual was born and spent both their childhood and adulthood.

A key set of studies of interest to wider demography is Jean-Pierre Bocquet-Appel's work on the evidence for a Neolithic demographic transition based on the spatial temporal distribution of archaeological sites. The findings have been used to demonstrate the presence, expansion, and contraction of modern humans and Neanderthals in prehistoric Europe and to determine the density of these hunter-gatherers in relation to technical and climatic conditions.

Population geography or spatial demography

Demographers and geographers have worked together in recent time to develop models to explore the relationships between space, location, and movement of people. However, some argue that the origins of spatial thinking and analysis in demographic research can be traced back to at least the period of *la statistique morale* in early 19th-century France. These studies have traditionally focused on topics such as migration, urbanization, and rural depopulation, but also increasingly make use not only of demographic data, but also of social and economic measures of wealth, access to social and economic capital, inequalities, etc. in relation to spatial distribution. Many contemporary surveys, such as the Demographic and Health Surveys (DHS), the World Fertility Surveys (WFS), and the Multiple Indicator Cluster Surveys (MICS), now include spatial data.

These studies have been greatly enhanced in recent decades by the use of sophisticated computerized geographical information systems, or GIS. Satellite-based global positioning systems now allow users to plot coordinates for locations across the globe, while Google Earth, and its more sophisticated cousin Digital Earth, enables population statistics to be linked to other quantitative data with a visual representation of the space. Indeed it is these new technological developments which are driving current progress in the sub-discipline. New data formats will be tagged with both a geographic location and a time stamp, thus providing unparalleled spatial and temporal precision. A new generation of activity space studies are being developed which harness technologies such as accelerometers, GPS, and smart phones to continuously monitor people in places. Spatial demographers argue that such technological developments, as well as new spatio-temporal precision, have enormous potential to improve our functional understanding of human spatial behaviour, and to contribute to new ways of thinking about relative and absolute utilization of space. Researchers harnessing this exciting new technology are now challenged by the need to identify those research priorities which will best advance the applicability of spatial demography to pressing societal concerns. New research questions in the field thus address issues such as teenage pregnancy in the USA, child mortality in Accra (Ghana), segregation and health in Boston (Mass.), migration and rural livelihoods in Madagascar, and demographic correlates of crime in Chicago (Ill.). The *Journal of Spatial Demography* was launched in 2013.

Population studies

Population studies is an interdisciplinary area of study typically attracting those with backgrounds in demography, epidemiology, sociology, economics, population geography, anthropology, public health, and public policy. Broadly speaking it addresses the interaction of social, economic, and demographic variables. It is thus an extension of the conventional study of fertility, mortality, and migration. Major areas studied include broad population dynamics; fertility and family dynamics; health; ageing, longevity and mortality; socio-economic variation and inequality; migration; human capital and labour markets.

The Population Association of America was established in 1930 as a scientific, professional organization to promote the improvement, advancement, and progress through research of problems related to human populations. The US Association of Population Centers (APC) was founded in 1991 as an independent group of universities and research groups whose mission is to foster collaborative demographic research and data sharing, translate basic population research for public policy decision makers, and provide educational and training opportunities in population studies. Currently, over forty academic and private research institutions belong to the APC, undertaking a variety of research into such topics as retirement, minorities, health, ageing, migration, families, fertility, mortality, and population forecasting.

Social demography

Social demography explores the interaction of population and society, and may be seen as a merger between sociology and demography. It is suggested that the term social demography was first used in a 1963 paper by the American demographer Kingsley Davis. University courses in social demography commenced in the 1960s in the USA and the first textbook titled *Social Demography* was published in 1970, with a 1975 meeting at the University of Wisconsin claiming to be the first social demography conference.

Initial interest focused on topics such as residential segregation, unemployment, and income gaps between status groups. The Chicago School of Sociology used demographic data to support sociological claims of urban growth and population distribution by socio-economic status. Some researchers argue that it is closely akin to population studies, in part due to the influence of American sociologists Hauser and Duncan, who codified the connection of sociology and demography in their 1950s work *Population Studies*. Others argue that it has a clear aim involving a three-way approach—data collection and descriptive interpretation; theory development and model testing; and contextual analysis (Box 9).

Researchers using demographic variables and techniques to study such societal issues as ageing populations, inequality in mortality rates, and differential fertility patterns may be classified as social demographers.

Box 9 What is the difference between demography and population studies?

In many contemporary analyses the boundaries between demography and population studies are now increasingly blurred as demographers recognize the complex interactions between social, economic, and demographic variables. The difference is that while fertility, mortality, and migration are the focus of classical demography, within population studies they are 'downstream' of social and economic variables.

Chapter 10
Population policies and future challenges

Most countries in the world have implicit population policies, in that they recognize that some of their policies will have indirect demographic outcomes. Far fewer have direct population policies which explicitly aim to modify a demographic outcome (see Figure 9). In general terms population policies are those policies which aim to modify the growth rate, composition, or distribution of a population. The United Nations defines population policies as actions taken explicitly or implicitly by public authorities in order to prevent, delay, or address imbalances between demographic changes, on the one hand, and social, economic, or political goals, on the other. This includes both the intentions and objectives with respect to selected population parameters, and legal and programmatic measures adopted to influence such parameters. Within this category the UN identifies policies addressing such issues as population growth, including fertility rates and particularly fertility rates among adolescent girls, policies influencing the size of the working age population, and the health-related issues of life expectancy at birth, under-5 mortality, and maternal mortality. Other health issues are not typically regarded as population issues. In 2013 the issue of the level of violence against women was also added. Population policies thus address the development consequences of population dynamics before they unfold by adopting forwarding-looking and proactive policies based on foreseeable demographic trends.

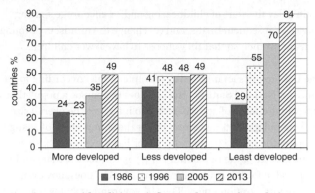

9. Governments with policies to influence the rate of population growth.

A population policy may thus aim to modify the growth rate, composition, or distribution of a national or sub-national population. These might be introduced if government felt that the population was growing or shrinking too fast, for example. A government might feel that the population had an unbalanced age structure—with too many or too few children, for example—or that its population was unevenly distributed across the nation, to the detriment of some areas which were either over- or underpopulated.

In practice population policies can be explicit or implicit. An explicit population policy is government action which explicitly aims at modifying a demographic outcome. This might be the imposition of a cap on immigration, subsidized family planning services, or a direct ban on couples having more than one or two children. An implicit population policy is government action which does not explicitly aim at modifying the population, but is understood to have a predictable demographic outcome. These might include, for example, introducing compulsory secondary education, which would (a) increase the average age of marriage and thus typically reduce age at first childbirth, (b) give women the skills they need to enter the economic labour market, and thus again delay the start of childbearing and/or encourage spacing between subsequent births, and (c) change the mindsets of young men and women so that they choose to have fewer children.

The UK provides an interesting example of this. According to its Office for National Statistics the UK 'does not pursue a population policy in the sense of actively trying to influence the overall size of the population, its age structure, or the components of change except in the field of immigration. Nor has it expressed a view about the size of the population, or its age structure, that would be desirable for the United Kingdom.' The UK does, however, have an immigration policy. The UK government states that 'immigration enriches our culture and strengthens our economy and therefore we want to attract people to study, work and invest in the UK'. The government thus aims to simplify and improve immigration policy and law, and ensure the UK has an internationally competitive visa system and an efficient and effective enforcement operation. It does this through carrying out immigration and customs checks to protect the UK border, efficiently processing applications for permission to enter and stay in the UK and applications to become a British citizen, and controlling migration to limit non-EU economic migrants and minimize abuse of all migration routes.

Fertility

There are many examples of governments which attempt to control the population's fertility. They may be direct population policies such as China's One-Child Policy or Romania's pro-natalist policies, or indirect such as Sweden's family policy.

One of the most famous population policies was China's One-Child Policy. This was a direct population policy aimed at reducing population growth through bringing down its total fertility rate. A voluntary policy in 1978, which aimed to curb the population as it raced towards 1 billion, was followed by the One-Child Policy in September 1980. A universal programme with exceptions for some ethnic minority groups and for those with a handicapped first child, it was implemented more effectively in the large cities of the east than in the small agricultural communities of the rural west. Various methods of enforcement were used, ranging from widespread availability of contraceptives and close community and workplace monitoring, through preferential employment opportunities and financial incentives for those who complied, to the more extreme measures of forced sterilizations and abortions.

The policy was effective in the areas in which it was enforced, resulting in a steady fall in birth rates to below replacement by the mid-1990s. However side consequences include a skewed ratio of men to women, as less valued baby girls were removed through abortion, abandonment, and infanticide, and the existence of possibly millions of unrecorded second and third children, who face a life without formal education, health care, or employment. In addition, the age dependency ratios within China's population have been exacerbated, as long-lived parents and grandparents find themselves without a nexus of children to care for them within the family. Recently couples where at least one parent is a one-child have been allowed to have two children, the majority of young adults now. However the indication is that most are choosing to stick to the one-child family model within which they themselves grew up.

In 1965, Romania, along with the majority of Central and Eastern European states, was in demographic decline, with a decline in births, and a TFR below replacement. The communist government under Nicolae Ceausescu believed that a large population was needed for military and industrial purposes. Concerned about the low rate of population growth, the Romanian government in 1966 introduced an explicit pro-natalist policy, including a number of measures to increase the fertility rate. These measures made abortion legally available only in certain limited circumstances, restricted access to contraception, and increased allowances for large families. The sudden imposition of severe restrictions on access to legal abortion and modern contraception had an immediate impact on fertility levels in Romania and the TFR rose from 1.95 to over 3 between 1965 and 1970.

However it then fell back over the subsequent decade to reach 2.25 in the 1980s. Given the perceived failure of the demographic policy, the Romanian government commenced a new campaign in 1984 to increase the birth rate and restrict abortion. Women of reproductive age were required to undergo regular gynaecological examinations at their place of employment. A special tax was levied on unmarried persons over 25 years of age, as well as on childless couples. And in 1985 the age required for a legal abortion was increased from 42 to 45 years or older, and a woman must have given birth to a minimum of five children who were currently under her care.

One of the first acts of the new transitional government of Romania in December 1989 was to repeal the aspects of the pro-natalist policy. However, due to the long prohibition on contraceptive use, many women lacked experience with modern methods of contraception and many members of the Romanian medical profession were reluctant to accept the safety of modern contraceptives. Despite this Romania's TFR fell during the 1990s and is now in line with other countries in Eastern and Central Europe at about 1.3 (see Figure 10).

Unlike the examples from China and Romania of explicit population policies, the example from Sweden is of an implicit population policy which does not explicitly aim at modifying the population, but is recognized to have a predictable demographic outcome.

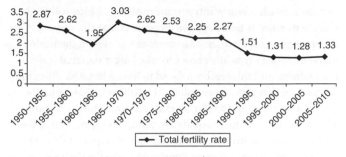

10. Total fertility rate Romania, 1950–2010.

While many European countries have seen their fertility continuously decline from the 1960s, the two-child family has remained a strong norm in Sweden, with few one-child families and a stable level of childlessness. However the total fertility rate of Sweden has continually gone up and down over that time. These ups and downs have been closely related to the economic business cycle and have been termed pro-cyclical fertility. Many have seen this related to Sweden's family policy, which has the basic aim of promoting good economic living conditions for all families and facilitating the combination of work and children for all women and men. Family policy goals are achieved by the widespread provision of day care centres and after-school services, parental insurance, and child allowance and other benefits.

Most young Swedish men and women become established in the labour market before they have children. Most women remain in the labour market after childbirth, and both men and women take a period of parental leave after the child is born. The parental leave system in Sweden is earnings related, and the benefit is dependent on recipients being active in labour market work prior to having children. Fertility went up at the end of the 1980s when the economy was strong and the length of parental leave was extended. During the 1990s the Swedish economy entered into a deep recession, young people became unemployed, and fertility went down.

However, Sweden is now introducing measures which will further enforce its aims. It has long been recognized that the very generous parental leave may disadvantage women in the labour market. Mothers typically choose to take longer parental leave than fathers, and this has been found to have a negative effect on women's careers and earning ability. In 2008 a 'gender equality bonus' was introduced to give an extra economic bonus to parents who share the leave more equally. Some are now questioning the decision, which is strongly promoting shared responsibility for children, rather than allowing families to make the decision on non-economic grounds.

Migration

The other main issue which governments attempt to control or influence though population polices is migration, both international and national (see Figure 11). Australia has long had a strong pro-immigration policy to build its country's numbers and labour force; it also until the late 20th century operated within this a policy which favoured European migrants. India has since Independence pursued policies which forcibly relocated

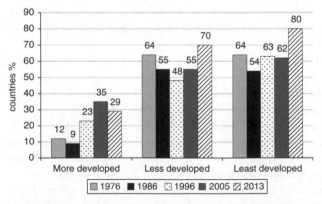

11. **Governments desiring major change in the spatial distribution of their population.**

numbers of its population, in order that industrial and other development projects might not be hindered.

Australia's current Migration Programme allows people from any country to apply to migrate to Australia, regardless of their ethnicity, culture, religion, or language, provided that they meet the criteria set out in law. At the last census (2011) Australia had 21.5 million residents, over one-quarter of whom were born overseas, and nearly half of whom were either born overseas or had a parent who was. As a country whose modern population was based on immigration, 20th-century Australian governments strongly encouraged immigration. However, in the first part of the century the country also pursued the so-called 'White Australia' policy, which placed restrictions on non-European migrants.

Following the Second World War, Australia took advantage of the instability and insecurity in Europe, and some Asian countries, to encourage refugees and displaced persons to migrate to Australia. Populating Australia was seen as a way of ensuring the country's safety and guaranteeing its economic future. Furthermore, it was argued that increasing the population would make Australia a less likely target for invasion. The White Australia policy was slowly dismantled after the Second World War and in 1966 the government announced that applications for migration would be accepted from well-qualified people on the basis of their suitability as settlers, their ability to integrate readily, and their possession of qualifications positively useful to Australia. The White Australia policy was completely removed by 1973 and in 1978 the government commissioned a comprehensive review of immigration in Australia. Far-reaching new policies and programmes were adopted as a framework for Australia's population development. They included three-year rolling programmes to replace the annual immigration targets of the past, a renewed commitment to apply immigration policies without racial discrimination, a more consistent and structured approach to migrant selection, and an emphasis on attracting people who would represent a positive gain to Australia.

India's resettlement and rehabilitation policies fall under the policy of 'development-related displacement'. Compulsory acquisition of land for large-scale projects such as dams, canals, thermal plants, industrial facilities, and mining frequently displaces people, forcing them to give up their home, assets, and means of livelihood. In recognition of the need to minimize large-scale displacement, and, where displacement is inevitable, to handle with care and forethought issues relating to resettlement and rehabilitation of project-affected families, the Department of Land Resources, Ministry of Rural Development formulated a National Policy on Resettlement and Rehabilitation for Project-Affected Families in 2003, with the objective of planning the resettlement and rehabilitation of affected peoples. In 2007 this was replaced by the National Policy on Resettlement and Rehabilitation, which aims at striking a balance between the need for land for developmental activities and, at the same time, protecting the interests of the landowners, tenants, the landless, the agricultural and non-agricultural labourers, artisans, and others whose livelihood depends on the land involved. It aims to minimize displacement and to ensure adequate rehabilitation occurs where displacement is necessary.

Future challenges

According to the United Nations, maximum world population will reach somewhere between 6 and 15 billion by 2100. The high variant 15 billion is generally recognized to place significant strain on the earth's resources. The medium variant 10 billion will be better but will still require a significant increase in the requirement for food, fresh water, energy, and minerals. In addition, the global distribution of people will also change, with an overall increase in those living in Asia and Africa, and a fall in European and North American populations. The less and least developed countries will account for 97 per cent of the growth to 2050. Asia will comprise 55 per cent of the world population by 2050 at 5 billion, Africa is projected to double in size by 2050 from 1 to 2 billion, while Europe will decline from 738 to 719 million. In addition the age composition of the population will also alter as median ages rise, and there is a proportionate shift from younger to older people across the globe. Around one-quarter of the world's population will be over 60 by 2050. Two-thirds of these will live in Asia which by then will have more people aged over 60 than under 15.

The magnitude and rapidity of these changes will raise considerable challenges for the 21st century.

Sub-Saharan African birth rates

World population growth over the rest of the century will be focused in Africa. While TFRs across the globe are generally falling, the case of sub-Saharan Africa remains of concern. The medium UN scenario is that TFR in Africa will fall to near replacement by 2050. If this occurs then the African population will increase from 800 million now, to 2 billion by 2050 and 3 billion by the end of the century. However TFR still remains above 4 in many countries. As a consequence if TFR reduction stalls and remains at its current 5.5 for the region, then SSA's population will reach just under 3 billion by 2050 and 14.5 billion by 2100, leading to a maximum world population of over 22 billion by the century's end.

The still high fertility rates and rapid population growth threaten the well-being of individuals and communities in the poorest developing countries, in particular those in sub-Saharan Africa. It is thus important that the drivers of fertility reduction are understood so that African women are able to choose the family size they desire. This is not only because a population of 22 billion would place considerable burden on the planet's resources, but because African governments increasingly recognize that such high birth rates are reducing the potential for development, and African women are themselves calling for measures which will improve their own well-being and those of their existing children, particularly the role that education and environment can play.

Feeding and providing water for the projected 9 or 10 billion by 2050

These two questions are still unanswered yet provide the 21st century with perhaps its biggest challenge. Around 884 million people are still without access to safe drinking water and 2.6 billion are without access to basic sanitation. Yet every baby born in the developed world consumes up to fifty times as much water as one born in the developing world. Some 1 billion people do not receive sufficient calories to meet their minimum dietary energy requirements and a further billion people are so chronically malnourished they do not get the vitamins, dietary minerals, essential fatty acids, and essential amino acids necessary for health. When we combine the predicted increases in population growth to 9 or 10 billion with the predicted and very necessary increases in calorific intake, we see a rise in total demand for food of 40 per cent by 2030 and 70 per cent by 2050.

The impact of the ageing of the world's population

The low fertility and low mortality rates for most countries are leading to an ageing of the world's population. Declining and ageing populations are often viewed as having dramatic negative effects on economic growth and employment due both to declining demand and to a declining workforce. The decline in the proportion of younger people in a population is perceived as leading to a reduction in economic activity and an increase in the proportion of older people, resulting in an economic burden through the higher requirement for pensions and health care. In particular the amount of ill-health and disability is likely to increase, the type of ill-health to change from acute to chronic conditions, and importantly, the effect of decreasing numbers of younger people will be to reduce those able to provide care.

The two main challenges facing high-income countries in the light of their ageing populations are how to ensure an income for these older populations, whether from work, pensions, assets, or savings, and how to provide appropriate and sustainable health care.

Already pension and health care provision accounts for up to 40 per cent of all government spending in advanced economies. One approach to the health challenge is to maintain health among older populations for as long as possible, thus reducing the requirement to provide and finance long-term health and social care, and sustain individual well-being. A second approach focuses on the economic factors, with populations working longer into old age.

The relationship between environment, population, and consumption in different parts of the world

Many researchers feel that it is a combination of increasing population with increasing per capita consumption which is the biggest challenge. Of particular concern is the impact of global inequalities. Increased consumption is essential to raise their standard of living for the 2 billion who live in extreme poverty and/or malnourishment. Yet these are the very countries where the significant increases in population growth will occur. It will thus be important to reduce the material consumption of the developed world, for our planet is finite and will struggle to support the material and economic consumption demanded by the growth in living standards in the emerging, developing, and least developed regions of the world. Other researchers also argue that continued economic growth worldwide is unrealistic due to environmental and resource constraints, and that the ecosystems that have sustained our economies are collapsing under the demands of rising consumption.

Such are the undoubted challenges facing the human population around population growth and consumption that there has been a return by some to Malthus: the renewal of concerns over feeding the global population, for example. Demographic momentum requires significant increase in food production to feed the burgeoning population, with implications for resources; economic development has spread Western style diets which are not an efficient way of consuming the earth's resources as food; food production per acre is tailing off. Malthus constantly sought to emphasize the complexity of the interrelationships between population, environment, socio-economic structures, and policy responses. Perhaps the founder of demographic studies still has a message for modern day demographers.

The impact of technological change

The introduction of new technology has historically resulted in the creation of new jobs, rather than a reduction in employment opportunities. The industrial revolution, for example, replaced a relatively small number of skilled artisans with large numbers of less-skilled factory workers. However the 21st-century digital revolution is displacing low- and middle-skilled jobs, and providing a small number of new job opportunities mainly for relatively skilled workers. The intersection of technological change and demographic changes has particular implications for the growing number of young men and women of working age in the middle- and low-income countries. Here many of these countries have used the availability of cheap labour to attract offshoring of jobs from Europe and the USA. This has promoted rural–urban migration as young people have moved to the cities for manufacturing employment, which in turn has driven national consumption, enabling the development of local markets and a thriving service economy. This process is an essential part of the growing labour market needed to turn the youth bulge into the demographic dividend. However, with a predicted 25 per cent increase in the use of robotics for manufacturing over the next ten years, high-income countries will increasingly replace not only their own manufacturing jobs, but previously offshored jobs with automation.

Importance of integrating demography into economic and political understanding

It is now clear that the demographic structure of the country plays an important role in the varied regional and national economic growth and that the demographic transition has played as crucial a role in the process of human development. Economists have long argued that the demographic transition follows on from economic growth, as this was historically the case in Europe and North America. As regions across the world go through the demographic transition, it is now clear that the narrative is a more complex process and that demographic, political, and governance structures are all of importance. Indeed the demographic transition's implications for the economy may be greater than economic factors for the transition. Indeed it has only exceptionally been the case that economic growth has occurred without the prerequisite beneficial demographic change. Over the next decade some 2 billion new babies will be born, 2 billion children will need to commence school, and 1.2 billion young adults need to find work. This simple demographic fact has significant implications for our planet, its regions, and individual nations. Understanding the implications of this will be crucial to the success of the 21st century.

Importance of integrating demography into economic and political risk forecasting

Glossary

age heaping the misreporting of a preferred number as one's age or to round one's age to a number ending with the digits zero or five.

age–sex structure the composition of a population according to the number or proportion of males and females in each age category.

age-specific fertility rate the number of live births occurring to women of a particular age or age group per year, normally expressed per 1,000 women.

age-specific rate a rate calculated to express the incidence of a demographic process at a given age or within a specified age group, typically within five-year age groups.

age-structure effect the role played by the relative size of each age group in a population in determining the number of vital events over a particular period.

birth cohort a group of individuals born during a specified period of time, normally one calendar year or a number of years.

birth interval the interval between entry into sexual union and a first birth or between two successive births.

birth order the classification of births according to the number of previous births to the mother.

birth spacing deliberate action on the part of couples to space the births of their children at particular intervals.

carrying capacity the maximum number of persons sustainable in a given area.

cause-specific death rate the number of deaths attributable to a specified cause or group of causes during a year, expressed per 100,000 of the mid-year population.

census the total process of collection, compiling, and publishing data on the demographic, social, and economic situation of all persons in a specified territory at a particular time.

circular migration patterns of *migration* (q.v.) in which individuals or groups move away and then return to the place of origin.

closed population where there is no migration in or out of a population and thus population growth depends upon the difference between births and deaths.

cohabitation two persons living together in conjugal non-marital union.

cohort a group of persons who experience the same significant event in a particular time period.

cohort analysis demographic analysis using *cohorts* (q.v.) as the unit of study.

cohort effect the demographic behaviour of an individual at any time conditioned by the accumulated experience of the individual and shared with other members of the same cohort.

component methods methods of estimating the size and age–sex structure of a population through breaking down overall population change into its component parts of births, deaths, and migration.

crude rate a rate which consists of the ratio of the demographic events occurring in a specified period to the average total population in that period.

density of population a comparative measure of the number of people resident within a standard unit of area.

dependency rate the ratio of the economically dependent parts of the population to the productive part.

emigration the process of international migration from a nation.

emigration rate the ratio of the number of emigrants leaving a specified country or region within a given period to the average population in that period.

endogenous mortality mortality due to ageing or to congenital defects.

enumeration an operation designed to provide information about the members of a population. It represents the data collection phase of a census.

event history a detailed account of a person's experience of one or more demographic processes (see *life history*).

exogenous mortality mortality due to external causes, such as accidents and parasitic or infectious diseases.

family planning conscious effort of couples or individuals to control the number and spacing of births.

family reconstitution a technique of record linkage which consists of linking together the vital events recorded by a registration system in order to reconstitute the history of individual families.

fecundity the capacity to reproduce, which may or may not lead to childbearing.

fertility the childbearing performance of individuals, couples, groups, or populations.

gerontology the study of all aspects of ageing, individual and population, and its consequences.

growth rate the ratio of the total increase (or decrease) in a population during a given period to the average population in that period.

hazard function a mathematical representation of the chance of a non-renewable demographic event occurring at each age or duration.

hazard model the use of covariates to estimate the impact of various independent factors using the hazard function of a process as the dependent variable.

household one or more persons who make common provision for food and other essentials for living.

immigration international movement into a given territory from another country.

incidence rate the number of new cases of a disease occurring in a population during a specified period of observation divided by the average population during the period.

infant mortality mortality of live-born infants who have not reached their first birthday.

inmigration movement into an area from a different part of the same country.

intercensal a qualifier applied to the period between two censuses, and to measures and phenomena occurring in this period.

kinship the relationship based on real, putative, or fictive consanguinity.

life cycle the sequence of stages through which individuals pass beginning with birth and ending in death, or families beginning with formation and ending in dissolution.

life expectancy the average number of additional years a person would live if the mortality conditions implied by a particular life table applied. Life expectancy at age x is represented by ex and life expectancy at birth $e0$.

life history a detailed account of a person's experience of one or more demographic processes (see *event history*).

life table a detailed description of the mortality of a population giving the probability of dying at each age.

marital status the status of individuals with regard to marriage.

marriage the legal union of persons of opposite or (in some countries) same sex.

maternal mortality mortality from causes connected with pregnancy, labour, or the puerperium (lying-in period).

migration movement of individuals or groups which involves a permanent or semi-permanent change of usual residence.

migration model a theoretical construct, often expressed mathematically, which attempts to explain observed patterns of migration.

momentum the increase (or decrease) in population size which would occur if the fertility of a population changed immediately to the level which would just ensure the replacement of each generation.

morbidity the state of illness and disability in a population.

mortality the process whereby deaths occur in a population.

nationality characteristic of an individual indicating his or her citizenship of a particular nation.

natural fertility the fertility of populations whose members do not use contraception or induced abortion.

natural increase change in the size of a population produced by surplus (or deficit) of births over deaths in a given period.

net migration the difference between the number of persons moving into a specified area and the number leaving.

outmigration movement from a given area into another part of the same country. Outmigration is one of the components of internal migration. Whereas emigration refers to migration to a foreign country, outmigrant is used to refer to people leaving a given area and moving to another part of the same country.

parity the number of children previously born alive to a woman (or to a couple). Parity is also sometimes used to mean the number of previous confinements experienced by a woman.

parity-specific fertility rates rates relating births of a given order to women of a particular *parity* (q.v.), e.g. third births, divided by the number of women who have already had two children, 'two-parity women'.

period analysis demographic analysis which focuses on occurrences within a specified period, often one year. The synonyms current analysis and cross-sectional analysis are also used.

population dynamics the study of changes in population size and structure brought about by mortality, migration, and fertility.

population pyramid a double bar-chart showing the *age–sex structure* (q.v.) of a population.

prevalence rate a measure of *morbidity* (q.v.) during a specified period of time (period prevalence) or at a specified point in time (point prevalence).

projection the computation of future population size and characteristics based on assumptions about future trends in fertility, mortality, and migration. A distinction is made between a projection and a forecast, the latter implying an element of prediction while the former simply represents the working out of various hypothetical assumptions.

proximate determinants of fertility biological and behavioural factors which directly influence fertility, and through which social, economic, and other factors come to influence childbearing. The alternative term intermediate fertility variables is also used.

quantum the ultimate frequency with which a given event occurs to the members of a *cohort* (q.v.).

ratio methods methods of calculating population *projections* (q.v.) for subpopulations through the application of the proportion of the total population in each subgroup.

record linkage the compilation of a variety of information relating to a person or a marriage.

return migration migration in which an individual returns to a previous area of residence.

reverse survival the reconstruction of a population's age structure at an earlier date on the basis of its current age structure and given assumptions about the prevailing level of mortality.

sampling collecting data from a part of a population with a view to drawing inferences about the whole.

sex ratio the ratio, within a population, of the number of males to the number of females, or the ratio of events occurring to males divided by the number occurring to females.

standardization a technique used to enhance the comparability of data from different populations.

stratified sampling form of sampling in which the sampling frame is subdivided into strata and sampling is carried out independently in each stratum.

tempo timing of events within a particular *cohort* (q.v.).

total fertility rate (**TFR**) the sum of the age-specific fertility rates over the whole range of reproductive ages for a particular period (usually a year), generally the number of children a woman would have during her lifetime if she were to experience the fertility rates of the period at each age.

urbanization an increase in the proportion of a population living in urban areas.

vital event a major change in an individual's status which leads to a change in composition of the population.

working age population the population in the age groups from which the labour force is drawn. Definitions of these ages vary, but 15 to 64 is common for international comparisons.

zero population growth (**ZPG**) a situation in which the number of births in and immigrants to a population equal the number of deaths and emigrants from it.

References

Chapter 2: From 55,000 to 7 billion

Livi Bacci, M. (2017) *A Concise History of World Population*. 5th edition. Hoboken, NJ: John Wiley & Sons Ltd, p. 2.

Chapter 3: The fathers of demographic thought

Graunt, J. (1662) *Natural and Political Observations Made Upon the Bills of Mortality*. Available at: <http://www.edstephan.org/Graunt/bills.html>.

Glass, D. V. (1950) Graunt's life table. *Journal of the Institute of Actuaries (1886–1994)*, 76(1): 60–4.

Petty, W. (1662) Treatise of taxes and contributions. In *The Economic Writings of Sir William Petty*, vol. 1. London.

Newton, I. (1687) *Philosophiæ Naturalis Principia Mathematica*. London.

Price, R. (1789) A Discourse on the Love of Our Country. Delivered on 4 Nov. 1789, at the Meeting-house in the Old Jewry, to the Society for Commemorating the Revolution in Great Britain.

Mr Bayes and Mr Price (1763) An Essay towards Solving a Problem in the Doctrine of Chances By the Late Rev. Mr. Bayes, F. R. S. Communicated by Mr. Price, in a Letter to John Canton, A. M. F. R. S. *Phil. Trans.* 53: 370–418.

Burke, Edmund (1790) Reflections on the Revolution in France, And on the Proceedings in Certain Societies in London Relative to that Event. In a Letter Intended to Have Been Sent to a Gentleman in Paris (1 edn). London: J. Dodsley in Pall Mall.

Price, R. (1772) *Observations on Reversionary Payments: On Schemes for Providing Annuities for Widows, and for Persons in Old Age; on the Method of Calculating the Values of Assurances on Lives; and on the National Debt to which are Added Four Essays on Different Subjects in the Doctrine of Life-annuities and Political Arithmetick, Also an Appendix*...London.

Price, R. (1772) *An Appeal to the Public, on the Subject of the National Debt*. T. Cadell.

Malthus T. R. (1798) *An Essay on the Principle of Population*. Oxford World's Classics, ch. 2, p. 19.

Chapter 4: The entrance of statistics and mathematical models

Gompertz, B. (1825) On the nature of the function expressive of the law of human mortality, and on a new mode of determining the value of life contingencies. *Philosophical Transactions of the Royal Society*, 115: 513–85. doi:10.1098/rstl.1825.0026.

Galton, F. (1889) *Natural Inheritance*. London: Macmillan.

Pearson, K. (1892) *Grammar of Science*. London: Scott. 2nd edn, 1900; 3rd edn, 1911.

Pearson, K. (1893) Contributions to the mathematical theory of evolution. *Proceedings of the Royal Society of London*, 54: 329–33.

Fisher, R. A. (1956) *Statistical Methods and Scientific Inference*. Oxford: Hafner.

The Editors of Encyclopaedia Britannica (2017) Sir Ronald Aylmer Fisher. *Encyclopædia Britannica, inc*. <https://www.britannica.com/biography/Ronald-Aylmer-Fisher>.

Hajnal, J. (1955) The prospect for population forecasts. *Journal of the American Statistical Association*, 50 (270).

Hajnal, J. (1965) European marriage patterns in perspective. In D. V. Glass and D. E. Eversley (eds), *Population in History: Essays in Historical Demography*. Chicago: Aldine Publishing Company, pp. 101–43.

Coale, A. J., and Hoover, E. M. (1958) *Population Growth and Economic Development in Low-Income Countries*. Princeton: Princeton University Press.

Coale, A. J., and Demeny, P. (1966) *Regional Model Life Tables and Stable Populations*. Princeton: Princeton University Press.

Population Council (1970) *Manual for Surveys of Fertility and Family Planning: Knowledge, Attitudes and Practice*. New York: Population Council.

The Royal Society (2012) *People and the Planet*. The Royal Society Science Policy Centre report 01/12, London.

Chapter 5: The drivers

Ravenstein, E. (1885) The laws of migration. *Journal of the Statistical Society of London*, 48(2): 167–235. doi:10.2307/2979181.

Zelinsky, W. (1971) The hypothesis of the mobility transition. *Geographical Review*, 61(2): 219–49.

United Nations (2013) *The Millennium Development Goals Report 2013*. New York: United Nations.

Glass, D. V. (1950) Graunt's life table. *Journal of the Institute of Actuaries (1886–1994)*, 76(1): 60–4.

Christensen, K., Doblhammer, G., Rau, R., and Vaupel, J. W. (2009) Ageing populations: the challenges ahead. *The Lancet*, 374(9696): 1196–208.

Caldwell, J. (1980) Mass education as a determinant of the timing of fertility decline. *Population and Development Review*, 6(2): 225–55. doi:10.2307/1972729.

United Nations, Department of Economic and Social Affairs, Population Division (2015) *World Population Prospects: The 2015 Revision*.

Chapter 6: The demographic transition—centrepiece of demography

Thompson, W. S. (1929) Population. *American Journal of Sociology*, 34(6): 959–75. [A precursor on the debate pertaining to the phases of the transition.]

Davis, K. (1945) World population in transition. *Annals of the American Academy of Political and Social Science*, 237(1): 1–11.

Carr-Saunders, A. M. (1936) *World Population: Past Growth and Present*. Oxford: Clarendon Press.

Notestein, F. W. (1945) Population: the long view. In E. Schultz (ed.), *Food for the World*. Chicago: University of Chicago Press, pp. 36–57.

Lesthaeghe, R. (1977) *The Decline of Belgian Fertility, 1800–1970*. Princeton: Princeton University Press.

Chapter 7: A demographer's toolbox

Lotka, A. J. (1907) Relation between birth rates and death rates. *Science*, 26: 21-2. Reprinted in D. Smith and N. Keyfitz, *Mathematical Demography* (Berlin: Springer, 1977), 93-96.

Lee, R. D., and Carter, L. (1992) Modeling and forecasting the time series of U.S. mortality. *Journal of the American Statistical Association*, 87(419): 659-71.

Coale, A., and Trussell, T. (1974) Model fertility schedules: variations in the age structure of childbearing in human populations. *Population Index*, 40(2): 185-258.

Brass, W. (1975) *Methods for Estimating Fertility and Mortality from Limited and Defective Data*. Chapel Hill, NC: Laboratories for Population Statistics.

Chapter 8: Population pyramids and projections

Population pyramid, Angola 2010. Data source: United Nations (2015) *World Population Prospects: The 2015 Revision*.

UK population pyramids, 1950, 1980, and 2010. Data source: United Nations (2015) *World Population Prospects: The 2015 Revision*. Accessed 10 May 2017.

Lexis, W. (1880) La représentation graphique de la mortalité au moyen des points mortuaires. *Annales de démographie internationale*, 4: 297-324.

Gompertz, B. (1825) On the nature of the function expressive of the law of human mortality, and on a new mode of determining the value of life contingencies. *Philosophical Transactions of the Royal Society of London B: Biological Sciences*, 182: 513-85.

Leslie, P. H. (1945) On the use of matrices in certain population mathematics. *Biometrika*, 33(3): 183-212.

Wachter, K. W. (2014) *Essential Demographic Methods*. Cambridge, Mass.: Harvard University Press, p. 272.

Chapter 9: Sub-disciplines arise

National Research Council (US) Committee on Population (1997) *Between Zeus and the Salmon: The Biodemography of Longevity*, ed. K. W. Wachter and C. E. Finch. Washington, DC: National Academies Press (US).

National Research Council (US) Panel for the Workshop on the
    Biodemography of Fertility and Family Behavior (2003) *Offspring:
    Human Fertility Behavior in Biodemographic Perspective*, ed.
    K. W. Wachter and R. A. Bulatao. Washington, DC: National
    Academies Press (US).
Newton, G. (2011) *Family Reconstitution in an Urban Context: Some
    Observations and Methods*. Technical Report, University of
    Cambridge, CWPESH No. 12. Minor revisions Jan. 2013.
Dublin, L., and Lotka, A. (1925) On the true rate of natural increase.
    Journal of the American Statistical Association, 20(151): 305–39.
Bocquet-Appel, J. P. (2002) Paleoanthropological traces of Neolithic
    demographic transition. *Current Anthropology*, 43: 638–50.
Hauser, P. M., and Duncan, O. D. (1959) *The Study of Population: An
    Inventory and Appraisal*. Chicago: University of Chicago Press.

Chapter 10: Population policies and future challenges

Department of Economic and Social Affairs Population Division
    (2013) *World Population Policies*. <http://www.un.org/en/
    development/desa/population/publications/pdf/policy/WPP2013/
    wpp2013.pdf>.
United Nations, Department of Economic and Social Affairs, Population
    Division (2015) *World Population Prospects: The 2015 Revision*.
    Accessed 10 May 2017.

Guinness, P. and Nagle, G. (2011) *Igcse Geography*. London: Hodder Education.

Newbold, K.B. (2010) *Population Geography: Tools and Issues*. Lanham: Rowman and Littlefield.

Chapter 10: Population policies and future challenges

Further reading

Bloothooft, G., Christen, P., Mandemakers, K., Schraagen, M. (eds)
    (2016) *Population Reconstruction*. Berlin: Springer.
Dyson, T. (2010) *Population and Development: The Demographic
    Transition*. London: Zed Books.
Harper. S. (2016) *How Population Change Will Transform Our World*.
    Oxford: Oxford University Press.
Livi Bacci, M. (2012) *A Concise History of World Population*.
    Hoboken, NJ: Wiley-Blackwell, 5th revised edition.
Livi-Bacci, M. (2017) *Our Shrinking Planet*. New York: Polity.
Longford, Nicholas T. (2008) *Studying Human Populations:
    An Advanced Course in Statistics*. New York: Free Press.
Mayhew, R. (2014) *Malthus: The Life and Legacies of an Untimely
    Prophet*. Cambridge, Mass.: Harvard University Press.
Malthus, T. (2012) *An Essay on the Principle of Population*. York:
    Empire Books.
Poston, S., Dudley L., and Micklin, M. (eds) (2005) *Handbook of
    Population*. Berlin: Springer.
Rowland, D. T. (2003) *Demographic Methods and Concepts*. Oxford:
    Oxford University Press.
Tesárková, K. H., and Kurtinová, O. (2017) *Lexis in Demography*.
    Berlin: Springer.
United Nations, Department of Economic and Social Affairs, Population
    Division (2015) *World Population Prospects*.
Wachter, K. W. (2014) *Essential Demographic Methods*. Cambridge,
    Mass.: Harvard University Press.

Index

E

F

G

H

I

J

K

L

Index

Demography